Model Texts Primary Classroom Book 2

Written by
KAREN MONCRIEFFE

First Published
May 2009 in Great Britain by

PUBLISHING

© **Karen Moncrieffe 2009**

The moral right of the author has been asserted in accordance with the
Copyright, Designs and Patents Act 1988

A CIP record for this work is available from the British Library

ISBN-10: 1-905637-73-X
ISBN-13: 978-1-905637-73-7

Typeset by Educational Printing Services Limited

Educational Printing Services Limited

E-mail: enquiries@eprint.co.uk   Website: www.eprint.co.uk

INTRODUCTION

The model texts in this book provide a wide variety of examples of different texts, which the children can use to inspire their own writing. The texts are purposefully designed to exemplify specific components or aspects of particular text types.

Whole texts are usually provided, in preference to using extracts, as on the majority of occasions at the end of a unit of work, children are expected to write a complete text themselves.

The related success criteria needed for writing each particular text type is provided. In addition to this, there is an accompanying assessment sheet for children to use to develop understanding of how to improve their writing. This sheet can be used for either self or peer assessment.

Teachers should begin by exploring examples of each text type and use the success criteria to identify characteristic features of particular texts. Following this, the children should write their own texts. Ideas for writing are given in the teaching notes. Encourage the children to use self or peer assessment to judge the quality of their work. Whenever possible, the children should be given the chance to edit and improve their work following assessment. It is expected that in the majority of cases, this process of developing writing will take place over a period of a few weeks.

The use of model texts, success criteria and encouraging the use of self and peer assessment is based on the central principles of assessment for learning. This approach has been proved to significantly raise standards in children's writing.

In addition to providing examples of text types, the model texts can be used in many other ways. For example, the teacher could:
- Create comprehension questions linked to the text
- Divide the text into sections and ask the children to re-order it
- Study sentence structure – identifying simple and complex sentences
- Identify word types within the text such as adjectives, adverbs and so on
- Read and discuss the short stories
- Find ways to link the texts to other areas of the curriculum such as history, science or design technology
- Develop drama activities linked to the text, e.g. hot seating or using freeze frames where appropriate.

The teaching notes provide detailed advice on how individual texts could be used.

CONTENTS

YEAR 5

YEAR 6

NARRATIVE TEXTS

NON-FICTION TEXTS

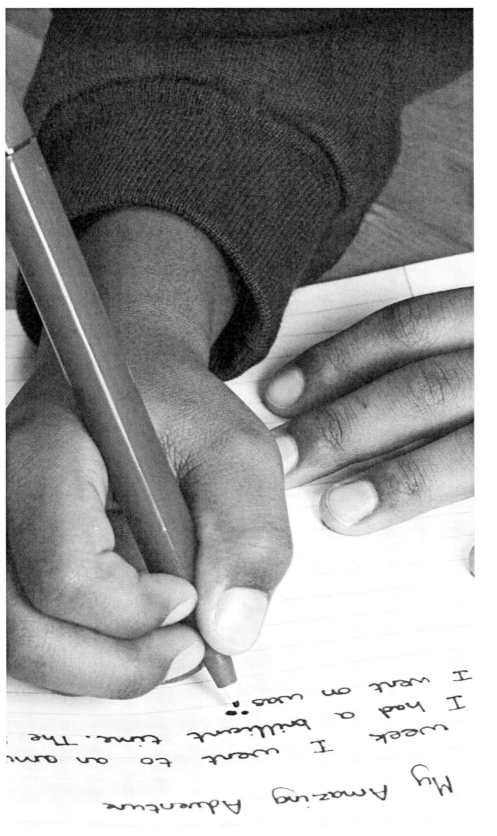

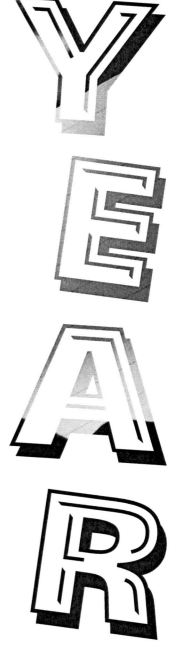

Teaching Notes: Year 5

Suggestions for using the model texts

As well as being exemplar texts for particular text types, the model texts can also be used as a stimulus for the children's own writing. Advice is given here on how the model texts can be used for this purpose and the appropriate Success Criteria (SC) and Assessment Sheets (AS) to use with them.

All About Me

Study stories written by the author Jacqueline Wilson. Identify elements of her style. Jacqueline Wilson usually writes realistic stories which are set in modern days and told in the first person. She has a unique approach to story writing and explores telling stories in a variety of different ways. For example, in *The Suitcase Kid* each chapter begins with a letter of the alphabet, and in *Double Act* the twins take turns writing entries to form an account of their lives. The model text is loosely linked to the format Jacqueline Wilson uses in *The Story of Tracey Beaker*. In this book the main character, Tracy Beaker, is asked to write a book about herself and her life. Using the subheadings in the model text as a basis, the children can write about themselves and their lives. The model text tells the story of an ordinary day in the life of the writer. However, the children could write about any significant day of their lives. For example, a family wedding, the day they moved house, an argument and so on.

Use SC and AS 1: *To write a recount.*

Fantasy Story Plan: Adventures in Argon

In contrast to Jacqueline Wilson's style, books written by significant authors such as CS Lewis delve into the world of fantasy. Explore the Narnia books written by CS Lewis or explore other popular fantasy novels such as those written by Phillip Pullman (*His Dark Materials* trilogy), *The Spiderwick Chronicles* by Holly Black or the popular *Harry Potter* series by J K Rowling. Discuss settings, characters and plotlines. Many of these books have been made into films so if possible; bring these stories to life by showing film extracts. The model text is a plan for a fantasy story. The children could use the subheadings to plan and write their own fantasy stories. Alternatively they could develop the ideas in the story plan into their own story.

Use SC and AS 2: *To write a fantasy story.*

Robin Hood

The model text tells the story of how Maid Marian came to join Robin and his group of Merry Men. There are many well-known tales that are associated with the legend of Robin Hood. Some of the tales are based on how Robin met some of the more famous outlaws included in his group of Merry Men. For example, there are stories linked to how he met Little John, Friar Tuck and Much the Miller's son. There are also stories linked to Allen-a-Dale, Sir Richard of Leigh and Robin's adversary Sir Guy of Gisbourne. A very popular tale is the story of Robin and the Golden Arrow. There is a wealth of information on Robin Hood to be found on the Internet, including versions of some of these stories. Ask the children to retell one of the adventures of Robin Hood.

Use SC and AS 3: *To write a legend*

The Sword in the Stone

The model text tells the story of the sword in the stone which introduces the legend of King Arthur. Research King Arthur and explore how the legend developed. There are many well-known stories associated with King Arthur, Merlin and the Knights of the Round Table. Some of these stories can be found on the Internet and there are many published versions of the Legend of King Arthur. Ask the children to retell one of these stories.
Use SC and AS 3: *To write a legend.*

Aladdin: A Mother's Tale

Aladdin is one of the stories that can be found in *1001 Arabian Nights*. These stories have existed for thousands of years, supposedly based on the legendary character Scheherazade, whom it is believed each night, told one of these stories to her cruel husband the Sultan, in order to spare her own life. Like Grimm's fairytales, the stories are not particularly designed for children; however, there are many child friendly versions of Aladdin. Tell the children the story of Aladdin and then ask them to retell it from a different perspective using first person. In the model example given, the story is told from the perspective of the mother. There are a variety of alternative perspectives that the children could use. For example, they could retell the story from the viewpoint of the Princess, the Sultan or even the genie in the lamp!
Use SC and AS 4: *To retell a story using first person.*

The Seventh Voyage of Sinbad

In *1001 Arabian Nights,* Sinbad tells the story of his seven voyages at sea. The model text retells the story of his seventh voyage. *Read and study some or all of the tales of Sinbad's other voyages. Discuss some of the key features of Sinbad's incredible adventures, e.g. gigantic animals, distant shores, being shipwrecked, finding precious jewels in strange locations. Ask the children to imagine that Sinbad embarked on an eighth voyage. Tell the children to write in first person and provide a recount of what happened.
Please note that in older versions of this story, voyage four contains some stereotypical ideas about people of different cultures. Teachers are advised to adapt the story as suitable or use a more modern version, possibly one adapted specifically for children.
Use SC and AS 4: *To retell a story using first person.*

Adding Dialogue: *Oliver Twist*

Oliver Twist is one of Charles Dickens' most famous novels. The scene where Oliver asks for more food is probably the most well-known part of the story. The model text is an example of how an extra scene of dialogue could be added to the original story and provides details of an imaginary conversation between Mr Bumble and Mr Limbkins after Oliver has dared to ask for more food. Read the first two chapters of *Oliver Twist* discussing the language and ideas in the story. Discuss how hungry the workhouse boys were and how it was decided that Oliver should be the one to ask. Explain to the children that they are going to write an additional scene of dialogue for the story, providing the details of the conversation between the workhouse boys as they discuss their hunger and try to work out who should be the one to ask for more gruel. Teachers may wish to enhance children's understanding of the story by using a video clip. There are many well-known film versions of the story.
Use SC and AS 5: *To write dialogue.*

Adding Dialogue: *Gulliver's Travels*

The story of *Gulliver's Travels* tells of the four imaginary voyages of Gulliver to fictional lands. The ideas contained within the story (for example, a land of little people, a land of giants) are very appealing to children. However, like many older stories which have become popular children's favourites, the story of Gulliver's travels was not specifically written for children, so teachers should check the version they are using for suitability. Despite the fact that the story was written hundreds of years ago, the style and language used by the author mean the text is fairly accessible and easy to understand even if an original version is used. Teachers should read and study with the children the whole of the story of Gulliver's first voyage to Lilliput before using the model text. The original story is written in the style of a first person recount and no dialogue is included. The model text adaptation looks at the opening part of Gulliver's first voyage. At the beginning of the story, when Gulliver wakes up on the beach, he is already tied to the ground with hundreds of pieces of string. The model text provides details of what may have happened leading up to this event with the emphasis on dialogue. The children could continue on from the model text up to the point where Gulliver wakes up, making sure they apply the appropriate rules of dialogue and write in the more formal style associated with older literature.
Use SC and AS 5: *To write dialogue.*

Polar Bear Mums: Video Narration

This is an imaginary example of a narrator's commentary of a TV documentary on polar bears. The children could write a similar narration for an animal documentary. This can be done by using a video clip of an animal documentary with the sound turned down. It would be good for the children to research their animal so they can describe fully what is happening in the video clip. The children will need to plan carefully using a storyboard and by paying attention to timings so that they can accurately describe what is going on at the appropriate times. Of course, any animal could be used for this work but a good alternative to the model text example is for the children to provide narration for a video on penguin dads. Teachers should work with the children to create the success criteria for the writing activity. Establish with the children that they must describe clearly what can be seen on the video in a way that will interest the viewer (think about use of vocabulary etc.). Remind children that without good use of punctuation the script cannot be read well. After the children have completed their writing they could perform their scripts in front of the rest of the class alongside the appropriate video clip. The class could evaluate each other's performances.
Use SC and AS 6: *To present a script to an audience.*

UK Weather Forecast

Show the children a TV weather forecast and discuss how it is presented. Talk about the symbols used on the weather map and specific vocabulary associated with the weather. Tell the children that they are going to present a weather forecast in front of members of the class. Explain that they will need to write the script first. Show the children the model text. Perhaps you could give the children a blank UK map and ask them to demonstrate understanding of the model text by plotting the appropriate symbols and locations in suitable positions. Following this, give the children another blank map, preferably A3 size, which they can use to create their own weather forecast. They should plot symbols and locations and create a script to go with it. Teachers should work with the children to create the Success Criteria for the writing activity. Establish with the children that they should describe clearly what can be seen on the map in a way that will interest the viewer (think about use of vocabulary etc.). Remind children that without good use of punctuation the script cannot be read well. The children should practise reading their script aloud, present their weather forecast in front of the class or a group, and then evaluate each other's performances.

Use SC and AS 6: *To present a script to an audience.*

BrekieBar Radio Advertisement Script

The model text is an example of a radio advertisement which contains a mini-play. Discuss different cereals and their qualities, ingredients used, and the supposed benefits of eating particular cereals as promoted by advertisers. Following this, the children could invent their own cereal and a radio advertisement for it. They could use a similar format to the model text with an introduction, a mini-play and concluding statement by the narrator. For example, a child eats the cereal before school and this leads to them doing well in a different subject; it could be winning a race in P.E., writing a fantastic story in English or getting full marks in a test. Teachers should work with the children to create the Success Criteria for the writing activity. As the advert contains a mini-play within it, remind the children of the conventions for writing a playscript. Also, discuss the elements of persuasive advertising – exaggeration, tempting descriptions etc. The children could work in groups, perform their adverts in front of the rest of the class and then evaluate each other's performances.

Use SC and AS 6: *To present a script to an audience.*

How to Make Cookies

If possible, demonstrate how to make cookies using the model text, or allow the children to follow the instructions to make the cookies themselves. Allow the children to evaluate the model text discussing how the instructions were written and whether they were easy to follow. Explain to the children that they will be writing instructions for how to make fairy cakes. The children could make notes whilst watching the teacher make fairy cakes and then write up the instructions. If possible, allow the children to make fairy cakes using the instructions they have written. Alternatively, instead of making fairy cakes the teacher could make something else, e.g. a sandwich or a smoothie.

Use SC and AS 7: *To write instructions.*

Children's Party Games

Explore the way the instructions are written in the model text – discuss layout, use of subheadings and sentence structure. The children could follow this by writing their own instructions for party games. Ask the class to discuss any other party games they know. If possible, allow the children to experiment with playing different party games before writing them up (this is useful if the children are unfamiliar with some of the games). Alternatively, the children could write instructions for playground games, card games or board games.

Use SC and AS 7: *To write instructions.*

Computers Made Simple

Explain to the children that this is an imaginary page from a book for people who are not sure how to use a computer. The model text details how to use an email. Tell the children they will be compiling a book which explains how to use Microsoft® Word®, for people who do not know how to use the program. The children could work individually. Alternatively, the children could work as a class or group on separate pages of the book. For example, one child could write about how to alter text changing font colour and size etc., another child could explain how to insert clipart, another how to edit and so on. Alternatively, the children could write instructions for using PowerPoint® or Excel®. At this stage of primary school the majority of children will be familiar with using the Microsoft® programs. However, it is likely that the teacher will need to recap how to perform certain functions and allow the children to spend some time exploring the program that they are going to write about.
Use SC and AS 7: *To write instructions.*

The Fairytale News

Explore various newspaper reports identifying key features, how they are set out, style, use of quotes etc. Show the children the model text. This is a page from an imaginary newspaper which contains reports based on fairytales. Explain to the class that they are going to write similar newspaper reports. A good starting point is for the children to write a follow up report to the main story on the model text linked to the well-known story of Cinderella. This story could have the headline 'Prince finds his dream girl'. Remind children of other fairy tales and suggest possible headlines. For example Frozen girl found in street *(The Little Matchgirl)*, Prince blinded in tower fall *(Rapunzel)* or Wolf goes on rampage *(The Three Little Pigs)*. Aim to get the children to focus on an event that occurs during the story rather than retelling the whole story. Remind them that a report is different from a story and that they should not begin the report with the words 'once upon a time'! An alternative to using fairytales as a basis for newspaper reports is to create a newspaper based on nursery rhymes. For example headlines like Humpty Dumpty Falls off Wall or Brother and Sister Injured (Jack and Jill) could be used.
Use SC and AS 8: *To write a newspaper report.*

An Interview with Elizabeth I

The majority of students will be familiar with the Tudors and some of the Tudor monarchs. Explain that the model text is an imaginary interview with Elizabeth I. Discuss the type of questions and answers which create an interesting interview. Tell the children that they will be writing a similar interview. The interview could be with another Tudor monarch, e.g. King Henry VIII or Edward VI. Or the children could write an interview with a famous historical figure linked to the period of history they are studying. It would be a good idea for the children to use drama techniques such as role play in pairs, or hot seating (with one child acting as the monarch and the remainder of the class asking questions) to generate ideas for the writing activity.
Use SC and AS 9: *To write an interview.*

Blue Team Win 3-2!

The following teaching ideas integrate P.E. with English. Show the children some newspaper reports from the sports pages of newspapers preferably football reports. Read and then discuss the model text. Explain to the children that they will be watching each other play a football match, interviewing members of the team and then writing a report. During the P.E. lesson divide the class into two so that one half of the class can watch the other half playing a short game of football. The observers should take notes and when the match finishes, interview two of the players in order to obtain quotes. Following this, the observers should swap places with the players and the children who were previously playing should then observe, take notes and then interview the new players. After the P.E. lesson all children should have enough information to write a newspaper report based on the match they have seen.

Use SC and AS 8: *To write a newspaper report.*

Redevelopment Letter

Study the model text and discuss the options for the proposed redevelopment. Consider the reasons people might have for choosing a children's park, a supermarket or a library. Explain to the children that they will be writing a reply that promotes one of the three options. They will need to persuade the council that their choice is the best one. If there is time, the children could write three different replies from people with different viewpoints on the best option for the redevelopment.

Use SC and AS 10: *To write a persuasive letter.*

Letters to the Editor

Talk about the letters page in a newspaper and the purpose of it. Explain that people write to newspapers in order to express their views and have them published. Discuss the fact that although people write letters addressed to the editor, the editor does not normally reply. Explain that often letters receive no reply, but that sometimes readers respond to each other. Tell the children that they will be writing replies to the letters in the model text expressing their opinions on the issues raised. The teacher will need to explain the protocol that readers use when responding to other letters in a newspaper, e.g. Dear Editor, I am writing in response to Mrs Emma Whitfield's letter about the summer holidays...

Use SC and AS 10: *To write a persuasive letter.*

Come to the Summer Fair!

Show the children the model text and ask the children to write a persuasive poster for a school event (real or imaginary). For example, the children could write a poster to advertise a school production, a book fair, sports day or an after school club.

Use SC and AS 11: *To write a persuasive poster.*

ALL ABOUT ME

My Name: Hannah Louise Smith

My Age: Nine years old – nearly ten.

My Family: I live with my mum and dad. I'm kind of an only child but I have two half sisters who sometimes visit on a Saturday. They're a lot older than me though. Michelle is twenty and Lauren is twenty-two. I love them to bits but they feel more like aunties than sisters.

My Friends: My best friend is called Priya. We're in the same class at school and we've known each other since Reception. Priya lives quite far away so I don't see her at weekends. I have lots of other friends at school – like Natalie, Shantelle, Jordan and Hardeep. Shantelle lives on the same street as me so we often play out on a Saturday.

My Likes:
Dancing – I go to a dance club on Saturday mornings. Jordan goes too.
Art – It's my favourite lesson. When I grow up I want to be an artist – or a dancer – I can't decide which.
Watching DVDs – I've got about twenty different DVDs to choose from! I usually ask for them at Christmas or on my birthday. I have a television that's also a DVD player in my bedroom.
Computers – I love going on the Internet, playing games and sending emails to my friends.

My Dislikes:
Football – My dad watches it all the time on TV – which means I end up having to watch it too.
Maths – I find it really hard – especially fractions which we did last week.
Dogs – When I was seven this huge dog started barking at me. So I made a mistake and ran. It chased me and jumped up on me. It didn't bite me – my dad says it just wanted to play but ever since then I've been scared of dogs.

A Day in My Life: Last Saturday morning, Dad took me to my dance class. My friend Jordan was there but we didn't get to speak much because she was in a different group from me. We practised our dances and then we had to perform in front of everyone. After each group performed, Mrs Haley (the dance teacher) asked the rest of the class to say what was good about each performance and what could be improved. I don't think Jordan was too pleased when I said that her group wasn't dancing in time to the music. But Mrs Haley said if we weren't honest with our assessments we wouldn't improve.

When I got home from dance class at about eleven-thirty, I asked Mum if I could go on the Internet for a while. Mum said no – she thinks I spend too much time on the computer. She suggested I read a book instead! I stomped upstairs and shut my bedroom door – firmly. Really, I wanted to slam it but the last time I did that I was banned from using the computer for a week.

At around one my big sister Michelle came round. From my room I heard her talking to Mum, so I turned the sound on my DVD down and crept out onto the hallway to listen to what she was saying. She was asking Mum if she could take me to the pictures. Mum replied saying something about 'my attitude' which I think was a bit of a cheek as I'd tried really hard not to show I was angry. I'd even made sure I didn't slam the door.

Anyway, Michelle managed to persuade Mum to let me go and we had a really good afternoon. Michelle is quite old for a sister, but we get on well and I can really talk to her. Sometimes she gives good advice. On the way home from the pictures she suggested that I apologise to Mum. At first I said 'What for?' but really, I knew I'd been a bit moody so I agreed.

When we got home I said sorry. Mum told me that she was worried I was spending too much time on the computer – and that from now on I'd only be allowed on for one hour each day, unless I had homework to do. Actually, I'm fine with that. At least I know I'll get some time on it each day.

In the evening Mum, Dad and I played Monopoly. Dad won. It was about eight o'clock when we finished playing and at the back of my mind I was thinking whether it would be a good idea to ask Mum if I could go on the computer. After all I hadn't had my hour yet. But in the end I decided it would be best to leave it. So I ended the evening by going up to my room and watching TV.

It was a good day – nothing special – just like any other Saturday really – but Saturdays are so much better than school days – don't you think?

FANTASY STORY PLAN: ADVENTURES IN ARGON

Plot Outline:

David's parents buy a new house that needs renovating, so he is sent to stay in his great aunt Gertrude's house for the summer. He climbs down the stairs of the cellar and steps into a magical fantasy world known as Argon – but when he turns round in the cellar, the stairs have disappeared. To return home he must find Estrava, the good fairy queen who has the power to grant wishes – but Estrava lives high in the mountains of Argon and there are many obstacles to overcome before he reaches her.

Characters:

Main character – David

Good characters – fairies, talking animals, Estrava.

Bad characters – dragons, giants, goblins.

Settings:

Great Aunt Gertrude's house

Fantasy Land – Argon

Beginning:

David arrives at Great Aunt Gertrude's house and begins exploring. His aunt warns him not to go down to the cellar because it can be dangerous – but he climbs down the stairs and enters the fantasy world of Argon.

Middle:

The fairies and talking animals (good characters) try to help David find Estrava but the bad characters try to obstruct him.

End:

David finally finds Estrava who grants him his wish to return home. When he returns home he discovers no time has passed and his great aunt is calling him for dinner!

ROBIN HOOD

The Legend Begins

Long ago, in medieval England, there lived a king who was fair and wise. This noble man was known as Good King Richard. He was respected and loved by all of his subjects. However, his duties extended far beyond the realms of his own kingdom and he left to do battle in the Holy Lands, leaving his brother Prince John in charge.

Unfortunately, Prince John did not possess the same good nature as his brother. He was an evil man capable of acts of great cruelty towards others. To make himself richer, he demanded that the poor people of the land pay taxes so high that many found themselves on the brink of starvation. Those who could not afford to pay lost their homes.

Prince John appointed men as dishonourable as himself to help him in his task. The Sheriff of Nottingham and Guy of Gisbourne were his most trusted allies. With their assistance, the rich people of the land became richer and the poor became poorer. For a time, it seemed as if there was little anyone could do to stop Prince John. Until the arrival of Robin Hood.

Who was Robin Hood? He was formerly known as Robin of Locksley until he suffered a fate common to many of his countrymen. Finding himself homeless after being cheated out of his father's land by Guy of Gisbourne, he disappeared into the depths of Sherwood Forest. Angry at the unfairness of a world where the rich could do as they liked while the poor suffered, Robin decided to fight back.

Rumours began of a man who robbed from the rich to give to the poor. A mystical figure, dressed in green so as to blend into the forest; at first, no one was sure of the truth of his existence. But as time passed, rich men would tell stories of being waylaid by a man wearing green, and being forced to hand over their cash. Poor people, often those in the most desperate of situations, about to be made homeless or without money or food, would receive surprise gifts. Money was left on their doorsteps or food delivered to their houses. Soon the truth became clear. No longer would the poor have to suffer without defence. No longer would Prince John reign supreme, with no one to prevent him doing as he wished. Help had arrived. At last there was someone who was brave enough to stand up to Prince John. And his name was Robin Hood.

Robin Meets Maid Marian

Of course, the legend tells not just of the story of Robin Hood, but also of his group of Merry Men. Inspired by Robin's bravery, other men who wished to fight against the unfair laws of the land soon headed to the forest to join him. Prince John was furious that anyone should dare defy him. Desperate to catch Robin and his growing group of Merry Men, he branded them outlaws and demanded that the Sheriff of Nottingham should consider it his top priority to capture them. But try as he might, the Sheriff had no success.

The forest was the domain of Robin and his comrades. Any foolish, wealthy person who dared to venture there would soon be 'relieved' of their goods – which would then be redistributed amongst the poor. And despite Prince John's growing fury, and the Sheriff's determination to find him, Robin continually evaded capture.

Robin and his men were constantly watchful and always on the look out for any visitors to the forest. So, when Robin was wandering through the forest one day and he saw a skinny looking boy with his face half covered by a hood, he stopped him demanding to know what business he had in the forest. In reply, the boy drew his sword and brandished it towards Robin. Surprised by this unexpected response, Robin's first instinct was to laugh. Did this boy not know who he was? Why on earth would a mere slip of a lad try to fight him? Did he not know he would lose?

A skilled swordsman, Robin expected an easy fight. However, it soon became clear that he had misjudged the feisty youth. Swords clashed back and forth as Robin battled with the youngster, and soon there were wounds on both sides. Robin found himself with a gash to his face and the boy ended up with a slashed arm. Blood dripped from both opponents. Still, the fight continued, until Robin, half weary, half admiring, called a halt to proceedings and declared a truce. At this, the youngster placed down his sword and pulled back his hood. And that was when Robin saw that this lad was not a lad but a young woman. And he realised that he knew her. Her name was Marian. He had known her for years – for she had been a neighbour of his. Or he had thought that he knew her. He had had no idea that she was so brave – or so capable a swordswoman.

Marian explained that she was in hiding, seeking refuge in the forest, because Robin's sworn enemy, Guy of Gisbourne, wished to marry her. And even worse – her father supported the union and insisted that she married him. Unable to see a way out of her predicament, Marian had fled. Impressed by her feistiness and attracted by her bold spirit, Robin soon decided that she was the woman for him. And it did not take long for Marian to realise that as much as Guy of Gisbourne had been the wrong man for her – Robin was the right one. And so the two became sweethearts and Marian became the only woman in Robin's merry group of outlaws. And she was as strong and skilful a fighter as any one of them.

THE SWORD IN THE STONE

In ages past, King Uther reigned over the Kingdom of England alongside his beautiful wife Igraine. The birth of their son filled them with joy. They named him Arthur and swore they would love and protect him forever. Unfortunately, King Uther had many enemies. Enemies he knew would not hesitate to kill him – or to kill his only son, Arthur, the heir to the throne.

And so King Uther and Duchess Igraine were forced to make the hardest decision of their lives. In order to ensure the safety of their son they entrusted him to the care of their friend Merlin, the magician. The son they loved was taken to a secret location and King Uther never saw him again.

Arthur was taken to the home of Sir Ector, an honourable man whom Merlin knew he could trust. Sir Ector raised Arthur as if he were his own son, never revealing the secret of his birth. So Arthur grew up believing Sir Ector was his father and that Sir Ector's son, Kay, was his older brother.

When King Uther died, leaving no obvious heir, there was great confusion. Who would rule over the land? Who should be king? Mysteriously, a magical stone suddenly appeared in the churchyard of St Paul's Cathedral. Sticking out of the stone was a sword. The stone bore the inscription:

Whoever pulls this sword out
of this stone is the true
King of England.

Lords and knights from all over the land tried, but none succeeded. Merlin the wizard had placed the sword in the stone knowing that only the hand of the rightful king would release it.

Kay, the son of Sir Ector was preparing for a jousting tournament and he'd agreed that his younger brother Arthur should act as his squire. Therefore it was Arthur's responsibility to bring all of the weapons needed. Kay was furious when he discovered that his younger brother had forgotten to bring his sword. How could he win the tournament without it? So Arthur was sent back to fetch it. Unfortunately, on reaching the lodgings in which they were staying, he found he could not gain access. No one was there and the doors and windows were securely bolted. Perhaps everyone had left to attend the tournament? A tournament his brother could not take part in without a sword.

Disheartened, Arthur walked slowly back to tell his brother the bad news. It was then that he saw it. Twinkling in the distance was a shiny silver sword sticking out of a stone. Arthur could not believe his luck. Running up to the stone he joyously pulled the sword out.

The monks who had sat guarding the stone could scarcely believe it. They had watched so many try and fail. Yet, standing in front of them, a skinny slip of a boy had effortlessly pulled the sword out of the stone. Respectfully they bowed before him. Arthur stood holding the sword wondering what they were doing. He decided he did not have the time to ask. Filled with urgency, desperate to get back to the tournament to give his brother the sword, he turned, about to run.

"Stop," one of the monks instructed, "read the stone."

Pausing, Arthur read the inscription. Stunned into silence, questions reverberated in his mind. Was it true? How could this be? How could he be the true king? In time, Merlin and Sir Ector would supply the answers. And in the years to come Arthur would prove to be one of the strongest, bravest kings that England had ever known.

ALADDIN: A MOTHER'S TALE

I am the mother of a sultan. Each day I dress in magnificent clothes, which are made from only the finest fabrics. I own more jewels than any one person could desire. My son is adored by the people of his kingdom for his gentle bearing, his bravery and his modest, courteous nature. Who would believe that my son was once a worthless, idle wretch of a boy who refused to learn a trade? A boy who wished for nothing more than to play in the streets all day long. I am the mother of Aladdin – and this is my story.

Aladdin's father, my husband Mustafa, was a poor tailor. Although we did not have much, we lived in peace and happiness for many years. However, as Aladdin became older his laziness became more apparent. My husband became so ill with worry over our son's slothful ways that he died. Yet, in spite of this, Aladdin did not change. Instead of working, he preferred to spend his time frolicking in the streets with boys as worthless as himself. Until one day something happened that was to change our lives beyond recognition.

The day started as any other, Aladdin was out wasting his time in the streets. I was at home trying to work out how to combine the scraps of food that we had into an evening meal. Suddenly, Aladdin came bursting through the door. He told me that he had met a man who claimed to be his father's brother. I remembered that Mustafa had once mentioned a brother whom I had never met. Using the meagre food that we had left, I managed to create an adequate meal and then instructed Aladdin to fetch his uncle so that he could dine with us. Aladdin returned with his uncle who brought with him a selection of wine and fruit which greatly added to our modest meal.

When the visitor questioned Aladdin about his trade, I was filled with shame on behalf of my son. Aladdin was forced to admit that he had no trade. With great sorrow, I explained to the visitor how my son cared for nothing but play. I was filled with joy when this seemingly benevolent uncle offered to buy Aladdin a shop and fill it with merchandise for him to sell. The next day, the man took Aladdin out and bought him a suit made of fine material. I was delighted to see Aladdin looking so splendid. The following day the man took Aladdin out again but I was worried when it reached night fall and they had not returned. Two days passed before I saw Aladdin again. To my surprise, I opened the door to find my son so weary and exhausted that he fainted on the doorstep.

When Aladdin came to, he explained that the man who claimed to be his uncle was in fact a wicked magician. The magician had given him a special ring and then made him go down into a magical cave in order to retrieve a lamp. Aladdin explained how he had hesitated momentarily when the magician had asked for the lamp. Because of this, the magician had flown into a fury and closed the entrance to the cave trapping him inside. Aladdin had grown so fretful alone in the darkness that he had clasped his hands together in fear and in doing so he had accidentally rubbed the ring. This had caused a genie to appear before him. The genie explained that he was a slave of the ring and would do anything the master of the ring asked. Aladdin had requested that the genie free him from the cave and this wish was granted.

Of course, after such an adventure my son was hungry and asked me for food. Sadly I had none to offer him. I had spun a little cotton and decided to go and sell that so that we would not starve. However, Aladdin had another idea. He had brought with him from the cave the dirty looking lamp that the magician had so desired. He decided to try to clean it and sell it. To our surprise, as he rubbed the lamp trying to remove some of the grime, a huge genie appeared. Later, Aladdin told me that this genie was thrice the size of the genie of the ring. I was so dumbstruck that I fainted. Undaunted, Aladdin boldly asked the genie to provide us with some food. When I came to, I saw that the genie had bestowed upon us an exquisite feast that was fit for a king. Tempted by this delicious banquet, I ate heartily and enjoyed the food that was offered. However, I had great reservations about using the lamp again. I worried that the genie may be evil, and begged Aladdin to sell it. He refused, deciding that he would keep the ring and the lamp and call upon the genies to do his bidding when needed.

And so it was for many years. Whenever we needed money or food the genies were there to provide. All was peaceful until one day Aladdin went out for a walk and returned home with some extraordinary news. He had seen the daughter of the Sultan and had instantly fallen in love with her. He wanted me to go and tell the Sultan that he desired his daughter's hand in marriage. At first, I burst out laughing. However, it soon became clear that my son was serious. Although I did not think Aladdin had a hope of his request being granted, I did as he wished. With the help of the genie of the lamp I obtained some magical fruit which sparkled like precious jewels. Then I made my way down to the palace. It took a few days of waiting patiently before I was granted an audience with the Sultan. When I told him of my son's love for the Princess at first he seemed unmoved and disinterested – until I showed him the contents of the napkin. Awestruck by the wondrous beauty of the fruit, he quickly agreed that his daughter could marry Aladdin. However, his official adviser, the Vizier, cautioned him against agreeing so impetuously and suggested that the Sultan allow a three month wait before the marriage went ahead.

I was unsure why there needed to be a three month wait but agreed to this request as in truth, despite the obvious quality of my offerings; I had not expected the Sultan to agree. I went home and told Aladdin the good news. However, just before the three months was up I was dismayed when I found out that the Sultan had broken his promise. I heard that the Princess was to marry the son of the Vizier. As the wedding was due to take place on the very night that I heard the news, there was little that could be done to prevent it.

At first Aladdin was upset when he heard the news but then he appeared thoughtful. He told me he had thought of a plan. The marriage took place, but on the eve of the ceremony, with the help of the genie of the lamp, Aladdin arranged for the bed containing the new bride and bridegroom to be transported through the sky to our house. I did not approve of Aladdin's plan but he went ahead with it all the same. I do not know the full details of what happened, but of course, the Princess and the Vizier's son were stupefied when they suddenly found themselves carried through the sky to a strange house by an enormous genie. They were beside themselves with terror when this happened on three consecutive nights. Quickly, the Vizier's son decided that, as a result of the strange goings on, he no longer wished to be married to the Princess and they were separated. This left the way clear for Aladdin.

Initially, the Sultan showed some reluctance to adhere to his earlier promise. However, after Aladdin showed the Sultan all of the riches he could provide the Princess he agreed. Of course, Aladdin never told the Sultan where the riches came from. Before marrying the Princess, Aladdin (with the help of the genies) built a sumptuous palace for her. They lived in the palace in love and happiness for many years. I watched my son change from a boy to a man. He was made Captain of the Sultan's armies and won many battles, but despite his bravery, he remained kind and courteous to all. For these reasons he was loved by the people of the kingdom and I feel the Sultan realised he had made a good choice in allowing his daughter to marry Aladdin.

All was well until one morning, whilst Aladdin was away on a hunting trip, to the astonishment of the entire kingdom, the palace simply disappeared! As the Princess disappeared at the same time, the Sultan surmised that his daughter had been inside. When Aladdin returned, the furious Sultan, distraught at the loss of his daughter, threatened to have him beheaded. Aladdin, unsure where the palace had gone, begged the Sultan for forty days to find her. I prayed for leniency and my wish was granted. Aladdin was allowed forty days to search for his wife.

Aladdin disappeared and I continued to pray hoping that Aladdin would return with the Princess. One morning I woke up and looking out of my window, to my surprise I saw that the palace had returned to its rightful place! Dashing over to it I found Aladdin there – with the Princess. My son explained how the evil magician, who so many years ago had pretended to be his uncle, had found out that he was married to the Princess. Jealous of his good fortune, the magician had used trickery to get his hands on the lamp and then spirited the palace away with the Princess inside. Using the power of the genie of the ring, Aladdin had found the palace with his wife inside. I asked him what had become of the evil magician, but he simply told me to worry no more as he was certain that the magician would never return.

Sometime later, I heard that the brother of the evil magician came looking for Aladdin. On hearing this, I was filled with great agitation as I knew that this brother was an evil and dangerous man. I rushed to the palace where Aladdin assured me that all was well. He told me that this brother had indeed turned up and that everything had been taken care of and there was no further cause for concern.

As far as I know this was true. Aladdin and the Princess lived in peace and tranquillity, without further problems, for many years. When the Sultan died Aladdin succeeded him and became Sultan himself. Many years ago, I only hoped that my son would learn a trade. Never did I dare to dream that one day he would become a king.

THE SEVENTH VOYAGE OF SINBAD

My name is Sinbad. I am one of the bravest sailors ever known. For many years, I sailed the seas. Each one of my voyages has been filled with excitement and adventure. Let me tell you the story of my seventh voyage.

I was onboard a ship in the China Sea when suddenly a violent storm developed. The waves rocked the boat from side to side and the crew began to panic. Then without warning, a gigantic whale, larger than fifty elephants, seemed to fly up from the waters towards the boat. Thinking quickly, I dived into the sea. I was just in time as the whale opened its enormous mouth and devoured the entire ship – including the rest of the crew!

Luckily, the whale swam off without seeing me. Eventually, the storm died down and I swam to the nearest shore. I found an exotic land full of tall trees and beautiful flowers. Soon I found a river and decided to follow it to see where it might lead. Using the wood of the forest I built a raft. Using the raft to navigate along the river was certainly easier than walking, but then disaster struck!

As I sat on the raft drifting along comfortably, a steep waterfall suddenly appeared before me. The raft plunged off the edge of the waterfall and I found myself hurtling downwards unable to hold on. For a brief moment, an image of my body impaled on the jagged rocks below flashed before my eyes. I knew that to land on those rocks would mean instant death. But to my surprise I felt myself land softly in some sort of net. The net was held by an old man who had been trying to catch fish. I bet he did not expect to catch a prize as big as I!

The old man was a good natured soul with a kind heart so he invited me to his house. And it was there I met his beautiful daughter Emira. We fell in love and she became my wife. I lived for a year on that island with Emira and her father after which time the old man died – leaving us both a fortune. After much consideration we decided to buy a boat and go sailing for a while.

We spent many months at sea visiting different places. And then as it always happens eventually, I felt the desire to return to my true home, the wonderful city of Baghdad. So here I am. My adventures at sea have made me a rich man. I am more than happy with my beautiful wife and my magnificent house.

And yet, some days I grow restless. Some days my heart yearns for more adventure. I wonder how long it will be before I take to the seas again....

ADDING DIALOGUE: *OLIVER TWIST**

"Oliver Twist has asked for more!" Mr Bumble explained breathlessly.

As soon as the words had passed Oliver's lips, Mr Bumble had rushed down to the boardroom to report him. Never in the history of the workhouse had this happened. Never before had a boy dared to ask for more food.

"What?!" shouted Mr Limbkins, an expression of shocked disbelief on his face.

"'Please, sir, I want some more', that's what he said," Mr Bumble repeated. "He was as brazen as could be!"

"You mean after he had eaten his gruel, he demanded more?" asked Mr Limbkins, still unable to believe any of the workhouse boys would have the audacity to commit such an offence. In all of the time that he had served as head of the workhouse, he had never known of anything as scandalous as this to happen.

"Yes, he walked right up to the front of the dining room and held out his bowl!" Mr Bumble elaborated, "Neither I nor the cook could believe what we were seeing!"

Mr Limbkins struggled to his feet. He was a large, round, red faced man who evidently had no idea what it was like to be so desperately hungry that you would be reduced to begging for another bowl of gruel. He banged the table in front of him so hard it shook. "Send the wretched child to solitary whilst we decide what we shall do with him," he ordered.

Mr Bumble dragged Oliver down to the dark lonely place known as solitary – a cold windowless empty room where a person had only their thoughts to keep them company. Slamming the door shut, he returned to the boardroom to discuss Oliver's fate.

"One thing's for certain, he won't be staying here!" Mr Limbkins declared. "He's a bad example to the others!"

"We could always sell him – see if we could get a fair price," Mr Bumble suggested. "I'm sure we'll find someone who's in need of a child labourer."

"An excellent idea!" agreed Mr Limbkins, "I'd say £5 seems like a fair price for a child."

*An adaptation of Charles Dickens' classic novel: *Oliver Twist*

ADDING DIALOGUE: *GULLIVER'S TRAVELS**

Throwing open the door, Skyresh Bolgolam bounded over towards the Emperor. The Emperor was surprised at his impropriety. Skyresh was his closest confidant, but nevertheless, the Emperor still expected him to demonstrate an appropriate degree of respect. He assumed that all of his subjects would at least show him the courtesy of knocking on the door before entering his chambers.

"How dare you enter without permission?!" the Emperor snapped.

"My deepest apologies, your majesty, but I have news of great urgency!" Skyresh replied breathlessly.

"What is it?" queried the Emperor. He had never seen Skyresh so agitated. The man was barely able to contain himself.

"There is a giant who is the size of a mountain lying on the beach!" Skyresh answered.

For a moment the Emperor thought he had misheard. Yet, Skyresh stood before him with an expression of complete seriousness. The Emperor wondered whether Skyresh had lost his mind. There was no doubt that the job of an admiral was a stressful one. Perhaps the pressures of his role had become too much and he could no longer cope. Whatever reason could there be for Skyresh to stand before him talking such nonsense?

"Don't be ridiculous Skyresh – giants do not exist – except perhaps in the realms of a child's imagination," replied the Emperor with a faint air of contempt.

"Your Majesty," Skyresh continued, ignoring the Emperor's expression of disbelief. "I promise you it is true – there have been several reported sightings and panic is beginning to spread. We must act quickly."

Realising that Skyresh was telling the truth the Emperor snapped into action.

"Call Lalcon and Balmuff!" he ordered referring to his two most trusted advisers, the chamberlain and the judge. "And notify General Limtoc. Tell him to prepare the army immediately and head down to the beach."

The Emperor knew that if these stories of a giant were true then it was best to be prepared. However, he had no idea whether the Lilliputian army would be able to fight a giant.

*An adaptation of Jonathan Swift's classic novel: *Gulliver's Travels*

POLAR BEAR MUMS: VIDEO NARRATION

After five long months in hibernation, the mother bear's head emerges from the snow. She squints as her eyes become accustomed to the brightness of the spring sun. Carefully checking the surrounding slopes she makes sure the area is safe. Once she is certain that all is well, she climbs out of her snowy den and calls to her two cubs, signalling them to follow behind her.

For the cubs, this is their first glimpse of sunlight. They were born two months ago and have spent all of their young lives living in a hole in the earth beneath the Arctic snow. All the cubs have tasted so far is their mother's milk. They stare in wonder at their new environment. After weeks of confinement, they are unsure what to make of this strange new world. Seeking warmth and security, the cubs huddle into their mother's fur. Although the sun is shining, it is still bitterly cold. The temperature is minus thirty degrees. Soon, the mother bear and the cubs return to the comfort of their den.

A few days later, the mother and her cubs emerge again. The den may be comfortable, but the mother bear is weak. She has not eaten for five months and as a result she has lost half of her body weight. Now she is hungry and must find food. And so the family begin their perilous journey across the snowy slopes of the Arctic. It will not be easy. More than half of all polar bear cubs die in their first year.

The family have journeyed more than a mile from their den. There is no going back. The mother bear spots a breathing hole in the snow. The seals that swim in the water beneath the surface of the snow covered ice must pop out and take a breath of air every ten minutes. The mother bear waits by the breathing hole hoping to catch a seal cub. Soon, a seal cub pokes its head out of the hole. The mother bear pounces – but she is not fast enough and the startled seal cub manages to escape. As polar bears are large, slow, cumbersome creatures they have a success rate as small as five percent when hunting for prey.

After several misses, the hungry polar bear continues her journey with her cubs trailing behind her. By now she is starving, but her luck is about to change. Polar bears can smell a live seal from up to one metre under the ice. Suddenly, she stops and begins jumping heavily on the ice. Quickly crashing through, she grabs an unsuspecting seal cub. At last she has food to feed herself and her babies. The polar bear cubs will remain with their mother for two and a half years. During this time, the mother bear cares for them, protects them and teaches them how to hunt. She prepares them for life in one of the harshest environments in the world.

UK WEATHER FORECAST SCRIPT

Good morning and let's take a look at today's weather.

The day begins with persistent heavy rain to the north of the United Kingdom with Scotland experiencing strong winds which will clear to showers in the afternoon.

Over to the west, in Ireland, there will be rain and gusts of wind making for an unpleasant start although the dark skies will begin to brighten throughout the day.

Towards the eastern coast we have a slightly better outlook – with light winds, sunshine, a sprinkling of scattered showers and highs of eleven or twelve degrees Celsius. Down in the south there will be sunny intervals broken by isolated showers and temperatures rising to around fourteen degrees Celsius. Some central and eastern areas will remain dry.

So, overall, most parts of the UK will be sunny with the odd shower but it will be very wet and windy in the north and the west.

Moving onto the evening, expect a cold night with rain sweeping across most areas of the UK and low temperatures of around four or five degrees Celsius.

Have a good day.

BREKIEBAR RADIO ADVERTISEMENT SCRIPT

Narrator: Do your children sometimes miss out on having breakfast? All parents know that breakfast is the most important meal of the day – but if you find that you're often pushed for time in the mornings, what can you do? Why not try new BrekieBars?

Mini-Play

Mum: (*shouting*) Hurry up Timmy – we're going to be late!

Timmy: (*yelling*) I can't find my shoes!

Mum: They're in the hall!

Timmy: Thanks Mum! Have you seen my coat?

Mum: Look in the cupboard!

Timmy: Thanks Mum!

Mum: If we're going to get you to school on time we need to leave now!

Timmy: What about breakfast?

Mum: Don't worry – have one of these new BrekieBars. Eat it on the way to school. It's just like having breakfast.

Timmy: (*sound of opening bar and chewing*) Thanks Mum. Umm... It tastes delicious!

Narrator: Later that day at school.

Teacher: Who knows the answer to 16x6?

Timmy: 96!

Teacher: Well done Timmy! Who knows the answer to 24x5?

Timmy: 120

Teacher: Excellent Timmy. You're full of energy today!

Timmy: That's because I had a good breakfast, Miss!

Narrator: Tasty BrekieBars are packed full of nutrients and vitamins ensuring that your child has a healthy start to the day. BrekieBars come in a variety of flavours – choose from Strawberry Yoghurt, Nutty Vanilla and Fruity Surprise. Make sure that your child doesn't miss out on the most important meal of the day. Try new BrekieBars – and give your child the chance to shine!

HOW TO MAKE COOKIES

Ingredients
175 g plain flour
100 g butter or margarine
100 g caster sugar
1 medium sized egg
Half a teaspoon of vanilla essence

Equipment
2 baking trays
Bowls – one large and one small
Wooden spoon
Wire rack

> *** Top Tip:**
>
> Try adding 175 g of white or milk chocolate chips to the plain cookie mixture after you have added the flour.

1. Preheat your oven to Gas Mark 4, 350 °F, or 180 °C.
2. Prepare the two baking trays by greasing them with butter or margarine. Alternatively line your baking trays with greaseproof paper.
3. Place the sugar into the larger bowl and then add butter.
4. Using a wooden spoon, cream the butter and sugar together until smooth.
5. Break the egg into the smaller bowl and beat it. Add the vanilla essence and then transfer the egg into the larger bowl containing the sugar and butter.
6. Sift in the flour.*
7. Stir the mixture well.
8. Using a teaspoon place equal dollops of the cookie mixture onto the baking trays. (Make sure you leave space between each dollop).
9. Use the back of the teaspoon to flatten each cookie.
10. Bake the cookies for approximately 15 minutes.
11. Remove the cookies from the oven and place on the wire rack to cool.

> **SAFETY TIP** – Do not use your fingers as you may burn yourself – try using a spatula or ask an adult to help you.

CHILDREN'S PARTY GAMES

Musical Chairs

Count the number of children and then arrange chairs in two rows laying out one less chair than the amount of children. When the music starts the players should walk around the chairs. When the music stops each child needs to quickly sit on a chair. The child left without a chair is out. Remove a chair and restart the music. Continue until only one child remains. The remaining child is the winner.

Balloon Pass

Arrange the children into equal teams of six to ten. The children should stand in a line. Give the child at the head of each line a balloon. At the go signal, the balloon should be passed backwards, over the head of each team member until it reaches the back. Then the team member at the back of the line should run to the front of the line and begin passing the balloon back again. Repeat until the team member who was originally at the front is there again. The first team to complete the rotation is the winner. The game could be played again with the balloon being passed between each player's legs.

Desert Islands

Count the number of children and then scatter sheets of newspaper on the floor laying out one less sheet than the amount of children. When the music starts the children should dance or move around the sheets. As soon as the music stops players should jump onto a piece of newspaper. The player left without a piece of paper to stand on is out. Remove a sheet of paper and continue. Repeat. The last remaining player is the winner. Hula hoops can be used as an alternative to newspaper for this game.

Pass the Parcel

Prepare a parcel with a small present inside wrapped up within several layers of paper. The children need to sit in a circle. When the music starts the children should begin passing the parcel around. When the music stops the child holding the parcel should remove a layer of paper. Restart the music and continue. The game is over when the final layer of paper is removed revealing the present. At this point the child holding the present gets to keep it!

Who Am I?

A child is chosen to leave the room. This child is to be given a secret identity by the other children. The identity must be well-known, such as a famous singer or footballer. When the child who has been chosen to leave is asked to return, they must try to guess their identity by asking questions. They must only ask questions which can be answered with yes or no. Allow the children to take turns playing this game. To make it harder, state that the children must guess their identity within ten questions.

Remember to buy prizes for the winners of the games!

COMPUTERS MADE SIMPLE

How to Send an Email

First of all you will need to select an email provider and register your details deciding what your email address and password will be. The password is a security feature ensuring that no one else has access to your emails. After completing this simple procedure you will be ready to send emails.

1. Sign in by entering your user name and password.
2. Select **new** – this indicates that you wish to write a new email to send.
3. Enter the email address of the person you are writing to.
4. Choose a subject or title for the email.
5. Type the email.
6. Press **send**.

Yes, it really is that simple! Once you're feeling confident you may wish to try using these additional features:

- Changing the font. Along the top of the email text box you will find symbols which indicate shortcuts which can be used to change the font and style of the email.
- Adding an attachment. You may see the word attachment (or attach) written on the toolbar, or a symbol that resembles a paperclip may be used. Press the word or symbol and follow the links to browse and choose the appropriate file that you wish to attach to your email. You can choose a file, picture or a photo. Once you have selected your file it will usually be displayed under the subject box with the paperclip symbol next to it. Then send your email as normal and the attachment will be sent along with it.

Soon you will find it's much easier to send a quick email than write a letter!

THE FAIRYTALE NEWS

Prince loses his dream girl

Prince Othorio of Castleton was left distraught on Tuesday night, when the beautiful girl, whom he had spent the evening dancing with at his birthday ball abruptly disappeared. Witnesses say the unknown girl ran out of the ball at midnight leaving the Prince inconsolable. One observer commented:

"He seemed to really like her. After she arrived he didn't dance with anyone else!"

Another said:

"It seemed as if he'd fallen in love with her straight away!"

Despite the fact that many of the other girls at the ball wished to dance with him, the Prince had focused all of his attention on the mystery girl. Onlookers say the girl appeared to panic when the clock struck twelve.

"Suddenly she pushed the Prince away and dashed towards the door. He was shouting after her to wait, but she just ran off!" explained Peter Sedgwick, a close friend of the Prince.

As the girl ran out of the room, she left behind a glass slipper. The Prince hopes that this vital clue will help him to find the girl of his dreams. A royal spokesman revealed:

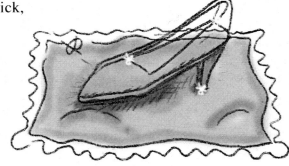

"Next week the Prince will begin a search for the owner of the glass slipper. All of the girls in Castleton will be invited to try the slipper on. He has decided he will marry whomever the slipper fits."

The Glass Slipper

MISSING BOY AND GIRL RETURN

Hansel and Gretel Smith, who have been missing for over two months, returned to their home yesterday. The children had been held captive in the home of an evil witch after becoming lost in the woods. Hansel explained how he had been trapped in a cage for much of the time. Commenting on his ordeal he said:

"It was horrible. I thought I was going to die!"

The children managed to escape from the witch after trapping her in an oven.

The children's father said: "I'm glad to have them home."

Hansel and Gretel

KING INVITES FROG FOR DINNER

Guests at a dinner party hosted by the King of Etherington were left stunned when he invited a frog to join them at the dinner table. A lady guest said:

"It was disgusting. It put me right off my food!"

Guests report that the King insisted that the frog sit next to his daughter and that the creature even ate off her plate. The King has refused to explain his actions simply saying:

"This is a private family matter."

AN INTERVIEW WITH ELIZABETH I

In 1558 Queen Elizabeth I came to power. At that time, many people did not believe that a woman could possess the skills or the strength needed to rule over the Kingdom of England. However, over time she proved all of her doubters wrong and became one of the most respected monarchs in British history. Below is an imaginary interview with Queen Elizabeth I after England's victory over the Spanish Armada in 1588.

How are you feeling after England's victory over the Spanish?
I'm delighted with the outcome of the battle. There was never any question in my mind that we would defeat the Spanish.

Some people have expressed the opinion that a woman is not strong enough to rule over England. Do you think you have proved them wrong?
Yes, I do. Anyone who still believes that I'm not capable of doing my job is a fool. I have more than proved my worth.

Do you feel that you are a better ruler than your father King Henry the VIII?
Let's just say we are different. He allowed himself to get distracted by matters of the heart. That will never happen to me!

Are you saying that you will never get married?
Oh, but I am married – to England! The country of England is the most important thing in the world to me. A husband could never compete with that!

Your father married six times. Was it difficult to deal with having so many stepmothers?
I really took no notice of many of my stepmothers. However, I was close to my father's last wife, Catherine of Parr. She was like a mother to me.

Do you have many memories of your own mother – Ann Boleyn?
I refuse to discuss my mother. The subject is off limits. Please move on.

What was King Henry like as a father?
I rarely saw my father when I was a child – except on special occasions like Christmas. It is common knowledge that my father wished for a son rather than a daughter. But in his own way, he was a good father. He ensured I received the finest education. The education I received was good preparation for my position on the throne.

Would you say you had a happy childhood?
I would much prefer to discuss matters related to today rather than the past.

Being queen of the country must be very stressful. What sort of things do you like to do in your spare time?

I enjoy riding my horses, hunting and archery.

Is it true that you have over 3,000 dresses?

I've never counted them but I do own a lot of dresses. I enjoy wearing beautiful clothes.

Are some of your dresses made with real gold and jewels?

Yes, that is true. I am the Queen and people expect me to look magnificent.

After the excitement of the Spanish Armada do you think you will take a holiday this year to relax?

I plan to travel around the countryside as I do every summer. It's so much better than being stuck in the palace all the time. And it gives people the opportunity to see me and hear what I have to say.

Thank you for being so open and honest your majesty.

You're welcome. As I've said – I believe it's important that my subjects should know their queen.

BLUE TEAM WIN 3-2!

On Wednesday 4th October, at 2.00 p.m., in the school hall, sixteen children in class 5 took part in a football match. The children were randomly divided into two teams of eight and given blue or red bands to wear in order to identify which team they were on.

Players were observed by the remaining fourteen members of the class. Mrs Garrety, the class teacher, acted as referee.

At the beginning of the match, Red team quickly surged ahead, with Robert Reeves confidently scoring a goal within minutes. In contrast, Blue team appeared disorganised and unsure, rarely managing to gain possession of the ball.

The outcome of the match seemed a foregone conclusion when one minute before half-time, Red team extended their lead, with Gurpreet Singh shooting a sensational goal from beyond the half way line, straight into the net.

During half-time Gurpreet said: "That was one of my best goals ever!"

The second half began with Red team winning 2-0. It seemed impossible that Blue team could win the match. However, an excellent goal by Keisha Brown changed the score to 2-1 and the fortunes of Blue team began to change.

After an aggressive tackle by Connor Smith, Red team were reduced to seven players, following the referee's decision to send him off. Blue team seized the opportunity to race ahead with Liam McDonald hammering home another goal for the team bringing the score to 2-2. Minutes later, Red team were ecstatic when Tyon Hughes scored. However, disappointment followed when the goal was disallowed.

With seconds to go, David Hodorowicz zoomed past several players in the Red team to score a brilliant goal, clinching a victory of 3-2 to the Blue team.

David said, "I think I scored a great goal and the Blue team were the best!" However, Gurpeet Singh disagreed, commenting, "I think Blue team were just lucky, but really Red team were more skilful."

Another member of the Red team also shared this view with Tyon Hughes saying, "If Connor hadn't been sent off and we'd had eight players then we would definitely have won!"

Reported by Fahim Khan

REDEVELOPMENT LETTER

Haddingway Council
High Street
H35 78Y

Wednesday 4th May

Dear Residents,

I am writing to discuss proposed changes to the wasteland area on the corner of Abbey Road. I am sure you would agree that at the moment this unattractive area is an embarrassing eyesore full of overgrown trees and litter. In its current state the area serves no purpose whatsoever.

I wish to invite all residents to express their opinions as to how the site should be redeveloped. At present, three ideas are being considered. The site could become a children's park, a large supermarket or a library – the final decision rests in your hands.

Please write to Haddingway Council Office, by Wednesday 24th June, expressing your point of view on this matter and detailing your reasons. The opinions of the community are of the utmost importance as we wish to develop the area in a way which best serves the local people.

We look forward to hearing from you.

Yours sincerely

T. Pritchard

Councillor Pritchard

LETTERS TO THE EDITOR

Express your opinion! Write to the editor at the following address: Heatherton News, Woodgate Street, Trenton Valley, T6 7RG. Or you can send your views by email to editor@heathertonnews.co.uk

Dear Editor

I wish to complain about children who wear clothing with hoods attached. Personally, I find this style of clothing quite intimidating.

The problem is that quite often you cannot see the full detail of the wearers' face; this means that a hood wearer could be up to all sorts and get away with it!

In my view these so called 'hoodies' are all trouble makers. I know this because there is a group of young hoodies who hang about by my local shops and they behave very badly.

I have a simple solution. Clothing with hoods should be banned. There is simply no reason for hoods. No one wore them when I was a child! If children's heads are cold then they should wear a nice woolly hat.

From Mr Tippery, Orton Street

Dear Editor

I wish to express my disgust over the fact that I have been fined £50 for dropping litter!

I believe that the fine was extremely unfair as it was only a crisp packet. I dropped it on the floor because I could not see a bin.

Obviously, no one likes litter but how could one crisp packet do any harm? In my opinion I did nothing wrong and I am sure that your readers will agree with me.

Yours sincerely

Sam Smith

Dear Editor

I would like to suggest that the government consider making the six week summer holidays a lot shorter. There are many reasons why I feel that this would be a good idea.

Firstly, I am certain that most children end up getting bored by the end of the summer holiday because it is so long.

Secondly, I am sure that many people would agree that it is a lot more peaceful when the children are at school. My next door neighbours have a six year old and an eight year old. They play in the garden all summer long and are extremely noisy.

Thirdly, I just don't understand why children need to have so much time off. It's not as if they have to work very hard at school! They spend most of their day sitting around listening to the teacher. What's difficult about that?

In my opinion children should only have two weeks' summer holiday a year.

Yours sincerely

Mrs Emma Whitfield

COME TO THE SUMMER FAIR!

The Brockfield Summer Fair begins at 1.30 p.m. on Friday 30th June. The event will help raise money for the school to buy new playground equipment. All sorts of exciting events will be taking place so don't miss out – make sure you're there!

- **Terrific toy stall** – Fantastic toys will be on sale for as little as 20p!
- **Brilliant bookstall** – Choose from an amazing variety of nearly new books.
- **Great games** – Can you throw a double and win a prize? Do you want to take a chance in our lucky dip? Can you shoot a basketball straight into the hoop? Choose from these games and many more!
- **Fun activities** – Pay 20p to throw a sponge at a teacher. Come on – you know you want to!
- ***Fantastic food*** – You will find a wide variety of healthy snacks available. Sandwiches, fruit and milkshakes will be on sale.

Please support the school by attending the School Fair.

SUCCESS CRITERIA 1:
TO WRITE A RECOUNT

- Write in the past tense.

- Use the first person.

- Use a range of sentence openers. Avoid starting every sentence with 'I'.

- Include details of Who? What? When? Where? Why? How?

- Write events in the order in which they happened*.

- Use new paragraphs to describe different events.

- Include interesting details.

- Use connectives that show time, e.g. after, when, following, later on, meanwhile.

- Use powerful verbs and adjectives.

- Describe feelings and emotions.

- End with a closing statement to finish off the recount.

*If appropriate, begin with an introduction explaining what the recount will be about.

SELF/PEER ASSESSMENT SHEET 1:
TO WRITE A RECOUNT

☐   Is the recount written in the past tense?

     Does the recount include details of:
☐   Who was involved?
☐   What happened?
☐   When it happened?
☐   Where it happened?
☐   How it happened?

☐   Are events written in order?

☐   Are new paragraphs used to describe different events or shifts in time?

☐   Does the recount include interesting details?

☐   Are connectives that signal changes in time used?
     e.g. next, later, after that etc.

☐   Are feelings about events and emotions (feeling sad, happy, excited etc.) identified?

☐   Is there a closing statement to end the recount?

     How could this recount be improved?

_____

_____

_____

_____

_____

_____

_____

SUCCESS CRITERIA 2:
TO WRITE A FANTASY STORY

- Plan your story carefully before writing.

- Set the main part of the story in a fantasy land.

- Have a clear idea of the plot. Decide why your main character is in the fantasy land. For example – are they on a quest? Do they need to find something or complete a task?

- Bring the fantasy land to life by describing in detail what it looks like.

- Include imaginary fantasy creatures such as dragons, monsters, fairies etc.

- Include vivid descriptions of imaginary creatures.

- Include lots of adjectives and adverbs to describe how your character is feeling at different parts of the story.

- Build the story up towards a climax (a really exciting part of the story).

- End the story with a resolution. For example, the main character completing the set task or good overcoming evil.

SELF/PEER ASSESSMENT SHEET 2:
TO WRITE A FANTASY STORY

- ☐ Is most of the story set in an imaginary land?

- ☐ Is the fantasy land described well – using lots of adjectives so the reader can imagine what it looks like?

- ☐ Does the story contain fantasy characters?

- ☐ Are the fantasy characters in the story described in detail?

- ☐ Does the plot make sense?

- ☐ Is it easy to understand what is happening in the story?

- ☐ Is there a really exciting part of the story?

- ☐ Does the story contain words which describe how the character is feeling?

- ☐ Is the problem in the story resolved at the end?

- ☐ Are paragraphs used?

- ☐ Is punctuation used properly? (Capitals, full stops, commas, speech marks etc.)

How could this work be improved?

_____

_____

_____

_____

_____

SUCCESS CRITERIA 3:
TO WRITE A LEGEND

- Use a story opener which shows the legend is centuries old. For example, Many years ago, Long, Long ago, In times past...

- Ensure the main character is special in some way. For example, brave, strong, clever etc.

- Show what the main character is like through their actions and dialogue.

- Use the opening of the story to introduce characters and setting.

- The middle of the story should contain a problem.

- Try to make the middle exciting.

- Describe in lots of detail how the problem is overcome.

- Use descriptive words and phrases to show how the main character feels at different points in the story.

- Make sure the problem is resolved at the end.

SELF/PEER ASSESSMENT SHEET 3:
TO WRITE A LEGEND

☐ Does the legend begin in a way that shows the story is centuries old? For example, Many years ago, In times past...

☐ Does the opening of the story provide information about the main character and the setting?

☐ Is the main character special in some way? For example, brave, strong, clever etc.

☐ Does the main character have to overcome a difficult problem?

☐ Is the middle part of the story exciting?

☐ Are lots of adjectives and adverbs used in the middle part of the story?

☐ Does the story contain words which show how the main character feels?

☐ Is punctuation used accurately?

☐ Are complex sentences used?

☐ Do sentences start in different ways, avoiding constant repetition of the main character's name or a pronoun (He or she)?

☐ Are paragraphs used?

How could this work be improved?

_____

_____

_____

SUCCESS CRITERIA 4:
TO RETELL A STORY USING FIRST PERSON

- Imagine you are a character from a story you have read or heard.

- Use the opening of the story to establish who you are.

- Write in first person using the word 'I'.

- Try to sound as if you are talking aloud to someone who is listening.

- Describe events in the story in detail.

- Include lots of adjectives and adverbs.

- Only describe the parts of the story that involve you.

- Use words to show how you feel about events in the story.

- Use sequencing words. For example, soon after, two days later, then...

- Use paragraphs to organise your writing.

- Include a wide variety of punctuation.

SELF/PEER ASSESSMENT SHEET 4:
RETELLING A STORY USING FIRST PERSON

☐ Is the story written in first person using the word 'I'?

☐ Does the writer pretend to be a character from the story?

☐ Are words used which show how the writer feels?

☐ Are events in the story described in detail?

☐ Are sequencing words used? For example, soon, the next day, then etc.

☐ Does the story only include details that involve the story character the writer is pretending to be?

☐ Are adjectives and adverbs used?

☐ Do sentences begin in lots of different ways avoiding continual repetition of the word I?

☐ Are paragraphs used?

☐ Is a wide variety of punctuation used?

How could this story be improved?

_____

_____

_____

_____

_____

_____

_____

SUCCESS CRITERIA 5:
TO WRITE DIALOGUE

- Use speech marks around spoken words: "........"

- Identify who is speaking before or after the character speaks, e.g.:
  Oliver said "Please Sir – Can I have some more?"
  "Please Sir – Can I have some more?" _said Oliver._

- Use a capital letter after the first speech mark.

- Use an appropriate punctuation mark before the last speech mark. This might be a comma, question mark, exclamation mark or full stop.

- Try using words other than _said_. For example, shouted, whispered, cried, asked etc.

- Try using adverbs or verbs in addition to _said_ to add interest, e.g.:
  "How dare you ask for more!" said Mr Bumble angrily.
  "But I felt hungry!" said Oliver trembling in fear.

- Each time someone different speaks, start a new line.

SELF/PEER ASSESSMENT SHEET 5:
TO WRITE DIALOGUE

☐   Are speech marks used around spoken words?

☐   Is it easy to identify who is speaking?

☐   Is a capital letter used after the first speech mark?

☐   Is a suitable punctuation mark used before the last speech mark?

☐   Have synonyms for <u>said</u> been used? e.g. shouted, cried, moaned.

☐   Have adverbs or verbs been used to add detail to how someone is speaking? For example:
"Stop it!" Emma shouted <u>angrily</u>.
"No I won't!" answered Mark <u>laughing</u> at her.

☐   Is a new line used every time someone new speaks?

How could this dialogue be improved?

_____

_____

_____

_____

_____

_____

_____

_____

SUCCESS CRITERIA 6:
TO PRESENT A SCRIPT TO AN AUDIENCE

- Make sure your voice is loud enough for the audience to hear you.

- Pronounce words properly.

- Pay attention to punctuation – stop and pause when necessary.

- Read fluently so that your words flow.

- Find the right pace – Make sure you are not too fast or too slow.

- Try to sound confident.

- Read with appropriate expression so that the listener is not bored by the tone of your voice.

- Practise first so that you don't make too many mistakes.

- If you make a mistake continue reading – don't panic.

- Don't giggle or laugh whilst reading your script (this shows you are nervous or embarrassed).

- Don't keep pausing and saying 'err....' or 'umm....' for no reason.

SELF/PEER ASSESSMENT SHEET 6:
TO PRESENT A SCRIPT TO AN AUDIENCE

Tick the boxes if the reader(s) of the script:

☐ Spoke loudly enough

☐ Pronounced each word clearly

☐ Read fluently

☐ Read at the right pace – not too fast or too slow

☐ Sounded confident

☐ Used expression

☐ Made hardly any mistakes

☐ Did not giggle or laugh while reading

☐ Did not keep saying 'err' or 'umm'

☐ Read fluently

Advice for the person (or people) who read the script:

_____

_____

_____

_____

_____

_____

SUCCESS CRITERIA 7:
TO WRITE INSTRUCTIONS

- Write the title.

- If the instructions need ingredients or equipment these should be listed at the beginning of the text.

- Decide how you are going to set out the instructions. Choose whether to use:
  - Numbered steps
  - Bullet points
  - Sequencing language, e.g. first, next, then, finally
  - Subheadings
  (You might use a mixture of these if appropriate)

- Try to explain as clearly as possible so that it is easy for the reader to follow your instructions.

- Use imperative verbs (bossy verbs), e.g. wash, slice, cut.

- Remember sentence punctuation – capital letters and full stops.

Optional Features:
To enhance the quality of your instructions you could include:
  - a short introduction
  - a 'Top Tips' section
  - a diagram to show each step or the finished product
  - an end statement.
However, these features are not essential.

SELF/PEER ASSESSMENT SHEET 7:
TO WRITE INSTRUCTIONS

☐   Is there a title?

☐   Is there a list of equipment or ingredients (if this is needed)?

Are the instructions set out in one or more of the following ways?
☐   -   numbered steps
☐   -   bullet points
☐   -   sequencing language, e.g. first, then etc.
☐   -   subheadings

☐   Are imperative (bossy) verbs used?

☐   Are sentences punctuated correctly using capital letters at the beginning and full stops at the end?

☐   Are the instructions written clearly and neatly?

☐   Are the instructions easy to understand?

☐   Are any optional features included? e.g. diagrams, top tips, short introduction, end statement.

How could these instructions be improved?

_____

_____

_____

_____

_____

_____

SUCCESS CRITERIA 8:
TO WRITE A NEWSPAPER REPORT

- Use large, bold writing for the headline (but don't go over the top and make the headline enormous!).

- Keep the headline fairly short.

- Write in the third person, e.g. he, she, it, they... (Not I).

- Include long complex sentences.

- Keep paragraphs fairly short.

- Use punctuation correctly, remembering capitals and full stops when necessary.

- In the first paragraph, summarise the main points of the newspaper article – What? Who? Where?

- In following paragraphs, provide more detail about the story – How? Why?

- Try to include quotes. Use speech marks.

- Explain what happened but make sure the report does not sound like a story.

Optional Features:
- you may wish to include a picture to go alongside your report but this is not essential
- you could set your report out in columns
- end with saying who reported the story.

SELF/PEER ASSESSMENT SHEET 8:
TO WRITE A NEWSPAPER REPORT

☐ Is the headline written in large, bold writing?

☐ Are paragraphs used?

☐ Does the first paragraph give the main facts?
i.e. What? Who? Where?

☐ Do the following paragraphs provide enough detail?
i.e. How? Why?

☐ Are most paragraphs fairly short?

☐ Are lots of long, complex sentences used?

☐ Are all sentences punctuated correctly, using capital letters
and full stops when necessary?

☐ Is the article written in the third person? (e.g. he, she, it,
they... not I)

☐ Does the report contain at least one quote using speech
marks?

☐ Does the article sound like a newspaper report rather than
a story?

How could the article be improved?

_____

_____

_____

_____

SUCCESS CRITERIA 9:
TO WRITE AN INTERVIEW

- Begin with a short introduction which gives a small amount of information about the interviewee.

- Identify the question and answer clearly. For example:
  - Write the question in bold (or use a different colour pen)
  - Write Q: before the question and A: before the answer

- Start a new line for each question and answer.

- Use a colon before the interviewer or person being interviewed speaks.

- The interviewer should avoid asking questions which can be answered with yes or no. Yes or no is a boring answer.

- Try asking questions that could lead to interesting detailed answers. For example:
  - How...?
  - Why...?
  - Do you think...?

- Do NOT use speech marks. They are not needed.

- Begin each sentence with a capital letter.

- Use a question mark for each question the interviewer asks.

- Use appropriate punctuation to end the sentences of the person being interviewed, e.g. full stop or exclamation mark.

- If necessary, use punctuation to show how an interviewee answers their question. For example:
  - Use commas, dashes or ellipses to indicate pauses.
  - Use brackets with verbs or adverbs before the words that they speak, e.g. (happily), (smiling), (irritated).

SELF/PEER ASSESSMENT SHEET 9:
TO WRITE AN INTERVIEW

☐ Does the interview include a short introduction?

☐ Is it easy to identify the question? (For example it may be written in bold/a different colour or begin with Q:)

☐ Is a new line used for each question and answer?

☐ Is a colon used before someone speaks?

☐ Does each sentence begin with a capital letter?

☐ Is a question mark used for each question?

☐ Is suitable punctuation used at the end of each of the interviewee's answers? (For example, full stops or exclamation marks.)

☐ Does the interviewer ask good questions?

☐ Are most questions followed by detailed answers? (Longer than three words – preferably a sentence or two.)

How could this work be improved?

_____

_____

_____

_____

_____

SUCCESS CRITERIA 10:
TO WRITE A PERSUASIVE LETTER

- Include your address (on the right) and the date.

- Begin your letter with Dear Sir/Madam or the person's name if you know it (remember to put a comma after).

- Use the first paragraph to explain why you are writing and to state your opinion.

- In the following paragraphs strengthen your argument by discussing the reasons you have for your beliefs.

- Use a separate paragraph to discuss and elaborate upon each reason.

- Use appropriate persuasive language, e.g. in my opinion..., my view is..., I believe...., surely... etc.

- Include complex sentences with a range of connectives, e.g. however, consequently, furthermore, in addition.

- In the last paragraph restate your opinion and make your position on the issue clear.

- Sign off appropriately, e.g. Yours sincerely if you know who you are writing to; Yours faithfully if you do not.

<u>Optional Features</u>
- Include rhetorical questions which have a seemingly obvious answer
- Use sequencing language like firstly, secondly etc. to discuss each of your reasons.

SELF/PEER ASSESSMENT SHEET 10:
TO WRITE A PERSUASIVE LETTER

☐ Is the address (on the right) and date included?

☐ Does the letter begin with Dear Sir/Madam or Dear followed by the person's name and a comma?

☐ Does the first paragraph explain clearly why the person is writing and state their opinion of the issue?

☐ Do following paragraphs provide reasons to back up the writer's opinion?

☐ Are separate paragraphs used to discuss each reason?

☐ Is persuasive language used? e.g. in my opinion..., my belief is..., my thoughts are...., surely etc.

☐ Are complex sentences with a range of connectives used? e.g. however, consequently, furthermore, in addition etc.

☐ Does the writer restate their opinion in the last paragraph?

☐ Does the letter end correctly? (Yours sincerely if writing to a named person; Yours faithfully if you are not.)

How could this letter be improved?

_____

_____

_____

_____

_____

_____

SUCCESS CRITERIA 11:
TO WRITE A PERSUASIVE POSTER

- Make sure your poster is attractive and easy to read.

- Use large clear writing or font for the title statement which identifies what the poster is about.

- Include different sizes and styles of writing for subheadings and information to make your poster more interesting.

- Include statements containing information.

- Consider using questions to engage the reader.

- Use second person, speaking directly to the reader, i.e. use you, your.

- Include language and phrases that appeal directly to the readers, e.g. don't miss out...make sure you're there!

- Use a range of punctuation.

- Include a picture or diagram to enhance presentation or provide more information.

SELF/PEER ASSESSMENT SHEET 11:
TO WRITE A PERSUASIVE POSTER

☐ Does the poster look attractive?

☐ Is large clear writing or font used for the title statement? (This shows what the poster is about.)

☐ Are different sizes and styles of writing used?

☐ Are there different statements containing written information?

☐ Is second person used to appeal directly to the reader, i.e. using you or your, as if speaking to them?

☐ Are questions used to engage the reader? e.g. How can you help? Did you know that...?

☐ Does the poster include language and phrases that appeal directly to the reader? e.g. Make sure you're there... Please support the school...

☐ Are pictures or diagrams used?

How could this work be improved?

_____

_____

_____

_____

_____

_____

Teaching Notes: Year 6

Suggestions for using the model texts

As well as being exemplar texts for particular text types, the model texts can also be used as a stimulus for the children's own writing. Advice is given here on how the model texts can be used for this purpose and the appropriate Success Criteria (SC) and Assessment Sheets (AS) to use with them.

Spooky Story

Use the model text to discuss some of the elements that should be included in a spooky story. Make reference to some of the suggestions given by the class teacher, Mrs Brennen, in the story. For example, discuss the types of characters, adjectives and adverbs that could be included in a spooky story. Identify how language is used in this story to build the tension. Discuss the ending of the story. Question the children – What might have happened in Kyle's nightmare? Remind them that Kyle described it as the most terrifying dream he'd ever had. Ask the children to write a spooky story entitled Kyle's Nightmare. The children should write the details of what might have happened in Kyle's dream including a story opening, a build up to a climax and a resolution. Although teachers often discourage children from ending stories with the character waking up to find 'it was all a dream', in this instance this ending would be an appropriate resolution to the story.
Use SC and AS 12: *To write a horror story.*

Alien Invasion

Discuss the genre of science fiction. Explain that science fiction stories are usually set in the future or in an alternative reality and that science fiction stories may have aliens or make reference to new technologies. Read the model text and discuss it. Explain that the story is set in the future. Question the children about what might have happened to Earth. Ask the children why they think the humans had to leave. If there is time, discuss environmental issues such as global warming, destruction of the rainforests and pollution. Ask the children to continue the story writing from the perspective of the humans who have arrived on Planet Una (perhaps in first person imagining they are one of the humans on the spaceship). Describe what the Unanians look like. How are they different to humans? What happens next in the story? Do the Unanians treat the humans well? Where do the humans live? Do the humans behave well on Planet Una? Do the humans like living on the new planet? The children could call their story 'Life on Una'.
Use SC and AS 13: *To write a science fiction story.*

The Trapper

Discuss what life was like for children in Victorian times and explain that many poor children had to work for a living doing horrible jobs. Talk about some of the different jobs poor Victorian children had to do, for example, working as a chimney sweep, working in factories or working in the mines. Read the model text. Tell the children they are going to imagine they are poor Victorian children who have to work for a living. Ask them to write a fictional recount of their day, describing what their job is, how hard the work is and their feelings about their life. It will be necessary for the children to do some research. Alternatively, if the children are studying or have recently studied a particular historical

period, they can write about a day in the life of a child from that era instead.
Use SC and AS 14: *To write a historical recount.*

The Stones of Asaria
Discuss the fantasy story genre and talk about fantasy books that are part of a series. For example, *The Chronicles of Narnia* by CS Lewis, *His Dark Materials* by Phillip Pullman, The *Harry Potter* books by J K Rowling and *The Spiderwick Chronicles* by Holly Black. Explain that writing a series requires careful planning. Explain that the model text is the beginning of a fantasy series of stories called The Stones of Asaria. Read the model text to the children. Tell the children they will be working in groups of four to complete the series. They must plan carefully what will happen in the series and how it will end. Following this, each child can work on an individual story. One child could continue the story entitled Diamond Quest, the other children can complete the other stories in the series (Sapphire Quest, Emerald Quest and Ruby Quest). Refer to the part of the story where Asaria and Horatio explain where each stone is hidden so that the children can base their stories around this. If there is time, the children could make their story into a simple book including book cover, blurb and illustrations.
Use SC and AS 2: *To write a fantasy story* (See Year 5 section).

Rainforest Quest
Read the model text up to the point where Tjan has to make a choice selecting from four different options. Explain that the story is an adventure quest where the reader's choice determines the outcome. If possible, show the children further examples of this type of story. Read the next part of the model text entitled Attack. Explain that this would be the ending to the story if the reader selected this option but that there are three other alternative endings. Tell the children they will be working in groups of three to write the remaining three endings for the story. If there is time, the teacher could extend this work by doing some work on rainforests and showing children some pictures. The more understanding the children have of rainforest life the better their writing will be. One child should work on Choice 2 – Hide, the other child on Choice 3 – Run, and the remaining child on Choice 4 – Approach. Explain that at least one of the choices should have a successful outcome. When the children have completed their work they could swap with another group of three and read each others stories trying to guess which choice will be successful.
Use SC and AS 15: *To write an adventure story.*

Keeping a Reading Journal
Tell the children they will be studying a novel by a significant author and making notes in a reading journal. Introduce the novel and show the children the model text. Explain to the children that they will be using the subheadings in the model text as a template for their own reading journal. Begin reading and studying the novel, making notes as indicated in the model text. Once the teacher has worked with the class to help them create a reading journal, the children should be able to repeat the activity independently. This means that the children should have the skills to understand how to keep a reading journal during guided or free reading if the teacher wishes. The children will need copies of the model text to guide them. The teacher should decide whether they would like the children to do

the suggested extension activities.
Use SC and AS 16: *To Keep a Reading Journal.*

Changes

Read the story and discuss the changes in Sacha's life. Remind the children that life is full of changes. Ask them to think about changes they may have experienced, for example, moving house, a new sibling, losing a pet, family changes etc. Teachers will need to be sensitive to the fact that some children may have experienced changes that have been traumatic and they may or may not wish to discuss them. Discuss how the story in the model text starts in the present, then moves back into the past (the memories of the main character) before returning back to the present again. Explain that this is a short story with a flashback. Ask the children to write a story where the main character has moved house and/or school. They should start in the present, flash back to the past (the main character could describe memories of their old house/school) and then move back to the present again at the end. The ending of the story should indicate a resolution where the main character shows they are beginning to adjust to the change in their life. Ask the children to think carefully about how they will show this. Does the main character begin to like their new house/school? Why? Do they make a new friend? Alternatively the children may wish to write a flashback story about another change.
Use SC and AS 17: *To write a story with a flashback.*

Duppy Island

This is an adventure story that does not follow the common story structure of opening – problem – resolution. Instead, it starts in the midst of the problem and then moves backwards to explain how the problem arose (flashback) before returning to the ending where the problem is resolved. Therefore the story structure is the problem – explanation of how the problem arose – resolution. Explain that this structure is used by authors to try to hook the reader in straight away so that they wonder what is happening and read on to find out. *Discuss the model text. Following this the children could write their own adventure story using a flashback. Suitable ideas could include the main character being trapped, maybe in a cave or a house or possibly lost in the woods. Suggest suitable beginning sentences for the children. Some ideas are given below:
"Help!" Mark shouted. No one answered....
It was so dark Akeem could hardly see. Suddenly he heard a noise behind him....
The children will need to plan their stories carefully first.
*Teachers may wish to extend children's understanding of the model text by discussing issues linked to slavery in the Caribbean further. For example, the children could investigate the Maroons (Jamaican slaves who escaped to the mountains of the island evading capture) and how or why all slaves were eventually freed.
Use SC and AS 17: *To write a story with a flashback.*

Why Was Gandhi Important?

Discuss the model text and how Gandhi helped change the world. *Tell the children they will be writing a biography of another famous person who helped to change the world. There are many significant people who the teachers could choose from, for example, Mother Teresa or Dr Barnardo. A good option for this work would be for the children to write about Martin Luther King. He is mentioned at the end of the model text because he was influenced by Gandhi. There are many similarities between the lives and beliefs of the two men. Teachers could compare what both men were fighting for and how they both believed in peaceful protest.

*Please note that it would probably be a good idea for the children to study this text and the following two texts on Gandhi *before* commencing work on writing their own biography of a famous figure.

Use SC and AS 18: *To write a biography.*

Significant Dates in the Life of Mahatma Gandhi

The model text is a simple list of important dates and events in the life of Mahatma Gandhi. Explain that date charts are suitable for quick reference and can often be found alongside a biography. There are several activities that could be done with the model text such as giving the children the text in the wrong order so they can sequence it correctly, or removing some of the dates or associated events so that the children have to do research to complete it. The children could then create a chart of significant dates for the famous person they are studying. Work with the children to create the success criteria for this simple text. Identify that the text must be in sequential order and that the significant dates are usually written in bold. Establish that the appropriate events are usually written alongside the date in note form or summarised in just one sentence.

(Work with the children to devise a suitable SC and AS for this work.)

Amritsar: An Imaginary Autobiographical Account

The model text is a fictional autobiographical account of one of the events that is mentioned in the biography of Gandhi. The children could imagine they were participants in The Salt March and write a recount of what they did, what they saw and what happened. They could also do similar work linked into the biography of the famous person they are studying. For example, they imagine they were a participant in one of Martin Luther King's marches or that they were there when he made his famous 'I have a dream' speech.

Use SC and AS 14: *To write a historical recount.*

City Children Arrive in Linley Hayes

Explain that the model text is an imaginary newspaper article from the time of World War II. Talk about what happened to the evacuees. Discuss how the same news can be reported in different ways. Tell the children they are going to write a newspaper report about evacuees from a slightly different perspective. Give the children the headline – City Children Sent to the Countryside – and tell them to write a similar article about the children leaving their city homes, including quotes from parents and children. Discuss how the parents and children might feel and what they might say.

Use SC and AS 8: *To write a newspaper report* (see Year 5 section).

Evacuee Interview

Explain that the model text is an imaginary interview with one of the children mentioned at the end of the newspaper report entitled *City Children Arrive in Linley Hayes*. The model text is an interview with one of the children who was not chosen by any of the villagers. Tell the children they are going to write a similar interview based on the same newspaper report. They could write an interview with a child who went to live with Mrs Eileen Milford or alternatively, the child who went to live with Mrs Evelyn Stauton. Discuss what it might have been like to live in the homes of both women. It would be useful for the children to do some drama perhaps in the form of hot seating or a role-play in pairs to enable them to think in more depth about the writing activity.

Use SC and AS 9: *To write an interview* (see Year 5 section).

Radio News Bulletin - The Birmingham Blitz

Explain that at the time of the Second World War many people in England listened to the radio (commonly referred to as the wireless) to find out what was happening in the news. And of course much of the news was centred on the war. Radio news bulletins usually began in the same way as the model text. 'This is the news...' followed by the name of the person reading it. Pick a significant event from the Second World War such as the day Britain declared war on Germany or Victory in Europe Day (VE day). Discuss the details of what happened and why. The children will need to do research or teachers will need to supply the children with appropriate information regarding these events. Following this, ask the children to prepare a radio news bulletin. Teachers should work with the children to create success criteria for the writing activity. Establish that the newsreader discusses who, what, where, when and why in the first paragraph before giving a recount of events. Teachers could incorporate drama/speaking and listening into this activity by asking the children to read their radio news bulletin aloud to the class, or record themselves and evaluate their performances.

Use SC and AS 6: *To present a script to an audience* (see Year 5 section).

Should animals be allowed to perform in circuses?

The model text is a simple points of view chart with a space included for the children to write their own views. Discuss the issues raised in the model text. Explain to the children that they will be completing a similar chart discussing the question 'Should animals be kept in zoos?' Discuss the reasons for and against this and let the children state their viewpoints. The teacher could organise a class debate on the issue. Following this the children can complete the chart. If the teacher feels it is necessary, they could provide a template of the chart for the children.

Use SC and AS 19: *To construct a points of view chart.*

Should primary school pupils be allowed to bring mobile phones to school?

Discuss the model text. Following this the children could write a discussion text about another issue that is relevant to their lives. For example, they could write about one of the following:

Should school children have to wear a uniform?

Should school children have to do homework?

Should children be allowed to have a television in their bedrooms?

Should children be restricted to watching television only one hour a day?

Discuss and debate the chosen issue. Remind the children that a discussion text presents both points of view on a topic in a balanced way.

Use SC and AS 20: *To write a discussion text.*

T37: The Importance of Healthy Eating

Discuss the model text. Explain that the text is a persuasive argument text. Establish that the aim is to encourage children to eat healthily. Tell the children that they will be writing a persuasive argument text entitled The Importance of Exercise. Explain that the aim of the text is to persuade adults and children of the importance of exercise. The text should contain at least three reasons why it is good to exercise.

Use SC and AS 21: *To write a persuasive argument.*

A Guide to Trent Hill Primary School

Explain that the model text is a formal guide for parents who are considering sending their child to Trent Hill Primary. Establish that the aim is to provide information about the school and its facilities. Tell the children they are going to write a similar guide for their school. Reiterate that the guide should have an impersonal serious tone as it is aimed at providing information to parents. The guide should highlight the key features of the school and contain a detailed description of facilities within the school and how they are used. The children will need to think about the layout of their school and decide on the appropriate subheadings they will use before they begin.

Use SC and AS 22: *To write a formal text.*

A Visitor's Guide to Blackpool

This work has links with the geography topic 'Contrasting UK localities'. After reading the model text, the children could write a guide for their local area or the city in which they live. Or they could write a guide for a different city or another popular tourist destination in the UK such as Brighton or Newquay. Explain that although visitors' guides can be persuasive, the aim of this guide is to supply information in a straightforward, impersonal way for visitors to the city.

Use SC and AS 22: *To write a formal text.*

SPOOKY STORY

"OK Class 6M. Listen carefully please. I need to tell you about your homework!" Mrs Brennen ordered her class.

Everyone groaned – except for Amanda Higgins who cheered. Kyle glared at her. He found Amanda very annoying. After all – who liked homework? She was just showing off because she found everything easy.

"Last week Amanda was our Writer of the Week with her fantastic story about the Vikings. Who will be Writer of the Week this time?" inquired Mrs Brennen.

Even though it was a rhetorical question, Amanda smiled complacently.

"Probably me again," she murmured smugly.

Kyle, hearing her, glared even more. She was so big-headed. Even more irritating, was the fact that she was probably right. He had to admit she was a great story writer. Kyle sighed. He had never been Writer of the Week. Unlike Amanda, he found story writing really difficult.

"I'd like you all to write a spooky story! Use your imagination and try to make it really scary!" Mrs Brennen explained.

The class stirred, becoming slightly more attentive. Many of them liked the idea of writing horror.

"Where will your story be set?" Mrs Brennen asked. "Maybe in a haunted house? Or in a cemetery? Or in the woods in the middle of the night?"

By now, everyone in the class was listening – ideas beginning to flitter through their heads. Even Kyle, was focused, his brow furrowed as he thought about the task.

"Why are you there? Are you lost? Is it a dare?" continued Mrs Brennen dramatically. "Who will your scary characters be? Ghosts? Monsters? Vampires? Werewolves?"

Class 6M suddenly sprang to life as all the children began to talk about their ideas at once. Mrs Brennen folded her arms and sighed loudly, waiting for silence. As the children noticed her annoyed expression a hush descended on the class.

"Thank you," said Mrs Brennen, "please let me finish before you discuss your ideas. Finally you'll need to think about what happens – make it exciting – build the tension. Make sure you use lots of adjectives and adverbs to describe your feelings.

The bell rang and Class 6M filed out of the room noisily.

As Kyle walked home he thought about what he could put in his story. To his surprise he was actually looking forward to doing his homework. As soon as he got home he grabbed a pen and paper. He wrote 'Spooky Story' at the top of the paper and underlined it. But half an hour later he'd written nothing else. Ideas whirred around in his head – but he just couldn't decide which to use.

Looking at the blank paper Kyle sighed. It was no good. Clearly, he was rubbish at story writing. Abandoning his efforts, he spent the rest of the evening watching TV. Soon it was time for bed. Covered by the cosy warmth of his duvet, Kyle stared up into the darkness. Even though he'd all but given up on his story, in the dark silence of the night, ideas began to drift through his mind.

As he slipped into sleep thoughts of vampires, ghosts, haunted houses, cemeteries and werewolves filled his mind. And then some of his thoughts became a dream and the dream became a nightmare....

Kyle woke up abruptly, his heart thudding so loudly it almost felt painful. He stared around him disorientated, unsure of where he was or what was going on. Fear enveloped him like a cloud. It seemed as if an evil presence was surrounding him. And then the feeling was gone. With relief, Kyle realised he'd been having a bad dream. In fact it was the most terrifying dream he'd ever had.

Gradually, Kyle's eyes adjusted to the darkness. Sitting up in bed, still feeling nervous, Kyle looked around his bedroom. As his gaze reached his bedroom door he gave a sharp intake of breath, too afraid to scream. Silhouetted in the doorway was the hazy shape of a headless boy floating in mid-air.

With his fingers shaking, Kyle reached out towards his bedside table, grasping frantically for the switch on his lamp. At last he found it. As he flicked it on light filled the room. At once he felt safe. He let out a sigh of relief as he realised his imagination had been playing tricks on him. The "headless boy" was nothing more than the shape of his school uniform hanging on his bedroom door.

Kyle looked at the clock. It was 3.00 a.m. Despite the fact that it was the early hours of the morning, Kyle didn't feel like sleeping. He thought about the horrible nightmare he'd been having before he woke up. What if he fell asleep and had the same dream again? Then suddenly Kyle had an idea. No longer feeling scared he grabbed the pen and paper from his bedside drawer. And then without a moment's hesitation, he began writing his story. His pen seemed to fly across the paper as he wrote down the details of his nightmare.

Two pages later, he'd finished. Sighing in self satisfaction he felt supremely confident. He doubted that anyone in class would be able to write a story that was as scary as the dream he'd just had. He smiled knowing that Amanda Biggins was going to be disappointed. Because this time, it was going to be his turn to be awarded Writer of the Week!

ALIEN INVASION

The spaceship looked like an enormous, sparkling, silver semi-sphere with an array of coloured glass windows scattered around its surface. The crowds that had gathered watched breathlessly as it floated towards the ground. A question that had existed since the beginning of time was about to be answered. Did aliens exist?

For many on the planet, the arrival of the spaceship confirmed something that they had always believed. They were not alone in the universe. Somewhere out there, distant galaxies existed containing life. Others stared at the apparition that had materialised before their eyes in disbelief, unable to convince their logical minds that this was really happening. But it was. An event was occurring which would change things forever. A spaceship was landing – right in the middle of the city.

An unidentified object had been spotted approaching the planet several days ago. As the object had neared, it had become clear that the object was some sort of spaceship. Scientists had plotted its course and correctly identified that the spaceship was approaching Iona City and would land in its centre sometime on Friday afternoon. As news had spread, the crowds had grown until a huge number stood ready and waiting – including the army and the planet's president Melitha Argo. Hopefully, whatever or whomever was on board would be friendly. But no one could guess what might be in store and the leaders felt it was best to be prepared.

The crowd covered their ears as the spaceship landed. The sound of its engines was as loud as a thousand pneumatic drills. Suddenly there was silence as the engines died and the crowd hushed in anticipation of what was going to happen – staring with a mixture of fear and excitement towards the spaceship's doors.

A few seconds later the door opened. Standing in the doorway were three strange creatures, the likes of which had never been seen. They stood upright on two spindly legs. Two arms appeared to protrude outwards from their shoulders. The skin on their faces was unnaturally smooth. Although the alien creatures looked similar, there were differences between them. It seemed the skins of this alien race came in varying shades of black, white and brown. Each alien appeared to have fur of different colours and textures springing from their head. The brown alien with short, black, shiny fur on the top of its head stepped forward and addressed the crowd in a loud voice stating:

"My name is Pedro and these are my friends Yasmin and Leon. More of my friends are inside the ship. We come in peace. Please do not be afraid."

Then the second alien stepped forward. The crowd stared in fascination at the silky yellow fur that sprung from the top of its head. They had never seen anything like it.

"We have journeyed for many years to reach your planet. Our planet has destroyed its resources. We have nowhere to live," the second alien explained.

Finally the remaining alien stepped forward and began speaking gently. The crowd stood transfixed, looking into the creature's large brown eyes.

"We are called humans. We are from Planet Earth. There are only a few members of our species left. We need your help. Could we please come and live on your planet?" implored the creature.

The inhabitants of Planet Una stared at the aliens experiencing a range of different emotions. Some felt sorry for the humans imagining how terrible it must have been to have to leave the planet on which they lived. Others felt angry. How dare these humans destroy their own planet and then expect to come and live on Una? Many eyed the human visitors with suspicion wondering if they could be trusted. Maybe the humans would destroy Una too (like they had done to their own planet). Maybe they were evil – perhaps they would try to take Una over.

But the crowd of Unanian inhabitants knew the final decision was not up to them. They turned to their president and waited for her to speak. President Melitha Argo wrapped her scaly, green hands around the microphone and held it to her lips to speak.

"Welcome to Una, earthlings," she said smiling. "This is now your home too."

And the humans breathed a sigh of relief, grateful that they had been given a second chance at life.

THE TRAPPER

"I want to go to school," I say loudly – although my voice is trembling.

My three brothers and two sisters stare at me as if I have taken leave of my senses. I look at my mother noting the expression of horror on her face. My father freezes half-way through putting the last pieces of coal on the fire. Angrily throwing down the coal, he spins round, his eyes sparkling with fury.

"School!" he shouts thunderously. "There will be no school for you. Do not talk of it again!"

And that is that. It is 1842 – Victorian England and no child would ever dream of defying their parents. My father has spoken. His word is law. I know I will never find the courage to ask him about it again.

Later, my mother takes me to one side of the dirty, rat-infested room that we call home.

"What are you thinking of Billy?" she asks me frowning. "School is not for the likes of us. We can't afford the pence fee – and we need the money from your wage."

"But I want to go – I want to learn new things." Finding a few remaining remnants of bravery, I manage to argue with my mother.

"Stop now, my boy!" snaps my mother. "Everyone in this family needs to earn their keep. How else can we afford to buy food? Now get some rest. You need to be up early for work."

Climbing into bed, barely able to find room squashed up against the bodies of my brothers and sisters, I try to sleep. But instead, I lie awake, unable to stop tears rolling down my face as I think about the depressing day ahead.

Soon it will be time to get up. In a few hours' time, I will be back at work again. I work as a trapper in the coal mines. It's one of the easier jobs so I suppose I shouldn't complain. I sit in the darkness by one of the doors in the underground tunnels of the mine holding a string attached to the door. Pulling on the string opens and closes the door which keeps the fresh air flowing. When I hear the sound of a coal wagon being pushed down the tunnel towards me, I open the door so it can pass. And that's it. That's all I have to do. For twelve hours a day – six days a week.

When I first started my job, I was six years old. I used to get scared sitting there in the pitch black silence on my own. I'm eight years old now – nearly nine, so I've been doing this job a long time. I'm not scared anymore but I hate it. Opening the door... closing the door... opening the door... closing the door. Can you die of boredom? Can you die of loneliness? There are times when I think I can't carry on any longer. When my mind starts screaming that I can't last till the end of my shift. But I have to – there is no choice.

You can't even risk falling asleep. My sister Annie used to work as a trapper, until she fell asleep and a wagon ran over her leg. She is lame now, so she doesn't work in the mines anymore. But she still works. All poor children do. She works from home with my mother making matchboxes.

I'm getter bigger now, stronger – so I won't have to be a trapper for much longer. Soon I will progress to being a hurrier. Like my brother David. He's ten. He wears a belt tied round his waist and there is a chain that passes between his legs which is attached to a wagon full of coal. He has to crouch down like a dog pulling the cart along behind him through the narrow wet tunnels to transport the coal to the surface of the mine. He says my job is not hard compared to his. And I believe him. So, soon I will become a hurrier like my David. And then after that, when I'm a lot older, I will become a miner like my two older brothers and my father.

One day a man came to the mines, he was dressed smartly – a rich man. But he was kind – not like most rich people. He spoke to me. Asking me questions about my job. How did I like it? When did I start doing it? And I told him what it was like, and how I hated it. He looked shocked and the expression on his face was sad. Shaking his head he said to me, "A smart boy like you should be at school". And then he left. That's when I started thinking about school – wishing I could go. I can read a little and write my name. The Sunday School teacher showed me how. She says I'm clever. That I'm a quick learner...

It seems like I've only just fallen asleep when I hear the voice of my father shouting, "Everyone up". It's time to go to work again and I feel like I've barely slept. Even though I am exhausted, I climb out of bed quickly. My father is waiting and he is not a patient man. There are no signs of daylight as we leave to make our way down to the mine. It is still in the early hours – four o'clock in the morning. Another day begins. I've heard talk that one day in England every child will get to go to school. That school will be free for all. But I don't believe that day will ever come.

THE STONES OF ASARIA

Prologue

Wizard Ondrec knelt on one knee before Asaria. Looking down at him, Asaria shifted awkwardly realising what he was about to say.

"Marry me!" said Wizard Ondrec. "Think how powerful we could be together. Let us join our kingdoms as one!"

Asaria averted her eyes away from his wrinkled face feeling embarrassed for him. She would have to let him down gently. In all honesty, she was amazed that he would have the audacity to think that there was even a small chance she would marry him. She was not attracted to him in the slightest. After all, he was an old man. Asaria was young and she wanted to marry someone who was more her own age. Besides, there had been no mention of love in Wizard Ondrec's proposal. The fact was that the wizard had no interest in love. He only cared about power.

Asaria was the Queen of the Kingdom of Goldecia. However, she did not insist that people refer to her as The Queen. Being a very modern ruler, she preferred people to call her by her first name. The wizard was the ruler of the nearby Kingdom of Poldez. He had gained his power after overcoming the previous ruler, King Horatio. To win the war against King Horatio he had used his magical powers, conjuring up evil spirits and monsters to help him gain control of the land.

Asaria knew that if Wizard Ondrec had wished so, he could easily have used his magical powers to gain control over Goldecia. However, Asaria was confident that he wouldn't be silly enough to try to do so. Although he was greedy, the wizard was not a complete fool. Clearly, he realised that, powerful as he was, it would be physically impossible for any one person to run two kingdoms. Yet despite this he still wanted more power. Asaria realised that his plan was to marry her so they could rule over both kingdoms together. She knew she would have to be tactful when she refused his offer. Wizard Ondrec was well-known for his bad temper.

"I like you a lot!" Asaria said carefully, "But I don't want to marry you. Can we just be friends?"

On hearing her words, Wizard Ondrec jumped up angrily.

"How dare you reject my proposal?" he shouted thunderously. "You will pay for this!"

Asaria's heart began to beat more quickly. The wizard looked absolutely furious. Nervously, she twisted the large ring on her finger. Immediately, she felt calmer. The magical ring had been in her family for generations. She was not a witch or a wizardess – but the ring gave her magical powers. The ring was the reason that her kingdom was such a wonderful place to live.

She ran her finger over the four precious stones. The blue sapphire gave her the power to make sure there was peace throughout the land. No one ever argued in Goldecia. The red ruby stone was linked to love. All Asaria had to do was touch the ruby stone and somewhere in her kingdom love would grow. In Goldecia, every one was happy with who they were and what they had. If any of her subjects showed signs of being jealous, Asaria would simply instruct them to touch the green emerald stone and any feelings of envy would disappear instantaneously. And each morning, Asaria would close her eyes and touch the precious diamond. The diamond was representative of wealth. Touching it each morning cast a magical spell across the land ensuring that no one in her kingdom was poor enough to be unhappy.

"I'm sorry!" Asaria said, determined to be firm," I don't love you, so I can't marry you, but as I've said – we can still be friends!"

"I don't want to be friends!" replied Wizard Ondrec angrily. "I don't even like you! I just want your kingdom!"

The wizard strode across the floor menacingly and grabbed Asaria's hand, wrenching the ring from her finger.

"Give it back to me!" shouted Asaria panicking. "The ring is useless in your hands. It's not magical unless it's in the hands of its rightful owner."

The wizard laughed dismissively.

"I don't want your silly ring!" he snarled. "I don't need a ring to do magic!"

And with that, he threw the ring up into the air. There was a flash of light and it disappeared.

"What have you done with it?" cried Asaria. Without the ring what would happen to her kingdom?

"The ring is gone and with it your power!" laughed the wizard. "The stones of the ring have been scattered throughout the land. And I have thrown the ring far, far away."

"Give me back my ring!" screamed Asaria frantically, hardly hearing what he was saying.

She lashed out at the wizard angrily, attempting to strike him. But he grabbed her arms calmly and smiled coldly at her.

"You know I could have made the ring disappear completely," he said coolly. "But this is much more fun. You will spend each day hoping that someone will find your precious ring, all the while knowing that the day may never come."

Asaria realised that she had probably lost the ring forever. As the wizard let go of her arms she sank miserably to the floor. She felt like she could hardly breathe.

"I told you that you would regret saying no to me!" snarled Wizard Ondrec, looking down at her contemptuously.

There was another flash of light and he disappeared.

Diamond Quest

Jemima emptied the contents of the silver jewellery box out on to the bed. When Great Aunt Cecilia had died she had left everything in the box to Jemima. She had died suddenly at the age of seventy-eight. Jemima's mum had told her there was no need to be sad about Aunt Cecilia's death as she had had a long and happy life. Still, Jemima felt a little bit sad as she sorted through the various items on her bed and thought about her great aunt. She had really liked her.

Aunt Cecilia had never married, preferring to travel the world instead. Jemima examined the different items on her bed. No doubt they were from countries all over the world. Picking up an old-looking silver ring, Jemima frowned, noticing that the stones of the ring were missing. She slipped the ring on her finger and looked at it. The ring didn't look very nice without the stones – she wondered where they were and why they had been taken out. Suddenly Jemima felt a whoosh and it seemed as if her body was being sucked backwards at great speed. The feeling lasted a few seconds and then stopped. Surprised, Jemima looked around her. She realised she was no longer in her bedroom.

She was standing in what appeared to be a castle. The walls of the room she stood in were slate-grey stone and adorned with various ornaments. In front of her stood a man dressed in similar clothes to a king she had once seen in a fairytale book. He looked as surprised as she felt.

"Jemima!" said the man smiling, seeming delighted at her appearance. "You're here at last!"

Before she could react, and ask him who he was – and how on earth he knew her name, a regally dressed woman and a young boy who was about the same age as her came running into the room.

"Jemima!" cried the woman enveloping her in a big hug. "I'm so pleased to meet you!"

"Who are you?" asked Jemima astonished by what was happening.

"My name is Asaria and this is my husband Horatio," explained the woman. "And this is our son Zenion," she continued pointing at the boy.

"What's going on?" Jemima demanded. Everyone around her was acting like this was completely normal – when clearly it wasn't.

"I'm sorry," said Asaria gently, "this must be a shock for you. Sit down. Let me explain why you are here."

Asaria pointed in the direction of a huge chair that looked like a throne. Not knowing what else to do Jemima sat down and listened as Asaria told her about the evil Wizard Ondrec and what he had done when she had refused his marriage proposal.

"This all happened twenty years ago," Asaria explained. "Life in Goldecia has been horrible since then. There has been war and fighting, and people being mean to each other. But I'm so glad I didn't marry Wizard Ondrec. I think things would have been worse than they are. I married Horatio instead."

"But I still don't know why I'm here!" Jemima said confused.

"Well you have my ring," Asaria said looking at Jemima's finger. "And I'm hoping you can help me get the stones. It's taken us a long time but we have found out exactly where Wizard Ondrec has hidden them."

"Where are they?" Jemima asked.

"The emerald is high up in the mountains in the north of Goldecia guarded by a silver dragon. The sapphire is in a cave close to the west coast of Goldecia – the cave is protected by goblins who work for Wizard Ondrec. And the diamond is somewhere in the Forest of Evil Spirits which is not too far from here," Asaria explained. "The ruby is the most important stone. But it will be the hardest stone to get – Wizard Ondrec has hidden it in his castle in the Kingdom of Poldez."

As Jemima listened incredulously, she wondered why they would assume that she would help them to get the stones. Making matters even worse Horatio added:

"This will be a difficult quest to complete. I wish that Asaria and I could go with you but as King and Queen of Goldecia we cannot leave the castle unattended. Without our presence the kingdom would fall further into disarray – perhaps irrevocably."

Jemima decided she'd heard enough. She could not believe what they expected of her. She had no intention of going anywhere near the frightening creatures they had told her about – and she had no intention of going anywhere near the terrible sounding Wizard Ondrec. She did not know why they thought she would help them. She just wanted to go home.

"I'm sorry," she interrupted, "but I don't know why you think I can do this."

"You can do it," insisted Asaria firmly, "your Aunt Cecilia told us you would help us."

"You've met my aunt?" Jemima asked shocked.

"Yes. She told us she'd found the ring in a place called Peru. She put the ring on just like you did and ended up here," Asaria explained.

"But that was eight years ago. She was seventy years old. She told us she was too old to help us but that one day she would give the ring to you and you would help."

Jemima wondered why Aunt Cecilia would have promised such a thing. Eight years ago Jemima had been two years old. Why had her aunt assumed that she would be brave enough to do this? As though reading her mind, Asaria answered:

"Your aunt told us that even then she could see that you had strength of character. She knew that you would grow up to be brave and strong."

Just then Zenion piped up interrupting his mother saying:

"She doesn't look very brave to me!"

"I'm tougher than you think!" Jemima shot back furiously. She glared at Zenion. Who did he think he was criticising her?

"So you'll help us then?" asked Asaria.

Asaria had waited many years for this moment. Looking into her hopeful eyes Jemima felt unable to disappoint her. Jemima thought about her Aunt Cecilia. Her aunt had believed in her. Maybe she *was* strong enough to do this.

"OK," agreed Jemima, "I'll help you find the stones."

"Thank you so much!" Asaria cried happily hugging her.

It all happened so quickly that Jemima scarcely had time to think. Looking towards the heavy wooden doors of the castle Jemima wondered what lay beyond. What did the strange, magical land of Goldecia look like? How could she have agreed to face horrible creatures like dragons and goblins when she was afraid of spiders?

"I can help you if you want," Zenion said. "You look like you need it!"

"That's a great idea!" agreed Horatio, "Zenion can show you where to go."

At first, Jemima wanted to refuse. She didn't want Zenion's help – he annoyed her. But then she reconsidered. If Zenion came with her then at least she wouldn't be completely on her own. So she nodded, agreeing to his offer of help.

"Well," said Zenion confidently, "where to first? The Forest of Evil Spirits isn't too far away. Shall we head there?"

"Lead the way!" replied Jemima trying to sound braver than she felt.

And the hunt for the missing diamond began.

RAINFOREST QUEST

Gently Tjan knocked on the door of his parents' room. He did not want his mother to hear him. She had already warned him not to go in.

"Your father needs to rest," she had told him.

But Tjan needed to see his father. To see for himself that he was alright. To spend time with him, just for a little while. As quietly as he could, Tjan turned the handle of the door and pushed it open. His father lay directly in front of him on a large bed in the middle of the room. Propped up on pillows, he lay motionless; his complexion was a sallow grey colour. His eyes were open as if smiling a silent welcome. Still, Tjan stood hesitantly at the door unsure whether to enter.

"It's OK," his father whispered so weakly Tjan could hardly hear him. "Come in... I want to see you."

Despite shutting the door as carefully as he could, the hinges made a slight creaking sound alerting his mother to his whereabouts. Suddenly she appeared, pushing open the door, not pleased at all to see her son in the room.

"Tjan please," his mother snapped, her voice both angry and weary at the same time. "Your father is very sick. Do not disturb him."

"It's... fine," his father interrupted quietly. The sound of his voice was ragged and breathless – as though it required a supreme effort just to utter a few words. "I want to see my son... after all... who knows how much time I have left?"

His mother's eyes filled with tears. Quietly, she closed the door, leaving Tjan alone with his father. Exhausted from his recent speech, Tjan's father said nothing else. Not wishing to weaken his father further, Tjan did not try to make conversation. Still, it was enough just to be near each other. After a few minutes, Tjan's father closed his eyes. Tjan leaned forward moving close enough to his father's face to feel his breath. Checking he was still breathing – still alive. And then he left the room.

Walking into the kitchen, he found his mother, standing by the stove stirring some soup, absentmindedly staring into space. Interrupting her sad thoughts, he gently called, "Mother?" and when she turned he walked towards her and hugged her.

"It will be OK," he said reassuringly.

His mother nodded and tried to smile. But the smile didn't reach her eyes. Because they both knew it wasn't true. His father was going to die. Silently, his mother continued stirring the soup. A few minutes later the soup was ready. Pouring it into a bowl, his mother placed it on a tray and took it in to his father.

Trying to help his mother in any way that he could, Tjan set about tidying the kitchen. But he was interrupted by a knock at the door. No doubt it was one of the village women bringing food, Tjan thought. The village of Yehmena was a close knit community and many of his neighbours had been saddened by the news of his father's illness and tried their best to help. But on opening the door, he found it was not one of the village women. Instead he found Ismaila, the local huntsman, talented, brave, rich and hated by everyone – for good reason.

"How is he?" Ismaila asked, in a voice filled with false concern.

"Not that you care – don't come here Ismaila. Go away!" snapped Tjan angrily.

"Come on...," said Ismaila smiling. " I'm here to help. For five hundred pesos I can give you the cure. You find the money – you save your father".

Ismaila was a skilled hunter. He wore the skin of a leopard draped over his back to prove it. The village of Yehmena was ten miles from the rainforest. Although the rainforest was not so far away, few of the villagers ventured there. It was a mysteriously beautiful place, with more exotic species of plants and animals than you could ever imagine. But it was a dangerous place where tigers, leopards and jaguars roamed free. In the depths of the jungle there were snakes that could swallow a man whole, and alligators with teeth as sharp as knives. Apart from the Qsari tribe, (rainforest people who lived deep in the rainforest, existing in harmony with its creatures) it was a place that few men dared to go. However, it was here that Ismaila hunted.

Traditionally, the people of Yehmena were simple farmers. Apart from Ismaila, few of the men were hunters. And none were as daring as he. Ismaila knew no fear. He would disappear for days hunting in the rainforest and then reappear with delicious tasting fruits and strange meats, which he would sell for extortionate prices. However, it was not selling these things that made Ismaila the richest man in the village. The most expensive item that he sold was a simple leaf. The leaf of the Bawaka tree. The medicinal properties of the Bawaka leaf had been known for centuries. When applied to wounds, healing would begin immediately. When boiled and given to those who were ill, their health would be restored. But it was a rare tree which only grew deep in the heart of the rainforest. And it was here that the most dangerous animals were. The leaf of the Bawaka tree was not easy to get. Many had tried to find it, but Ismaila was the only one who had had any success.

Suddenly Tjan was filled with desperation. To know that Ismaila had the power to cure his sick father was almost too much to bear. Forgetting any sense of pride, Tjan pleaded with Ismaila:

"We don't have the money. We are poor. But give me the leaf and I will work for you... for all of my life – I will do anything!"

Ismaila laughed dismissively, "What would I want with a little runt like you? It's money I want. Nothing else."

Tjan slammed the door shut furiously. For a few minutes afterwards he could hear Ismaila's laughter ringing in his ears. Then suddenly, his helpless anger was replaced with determination. He would go into the rainforest. He would find the Bawaka tree – and he would save his father.

* * * * * * * * *

In the early hours of the following morning, whilst his mother slept, Tjan quietly slipped out of the house. Armed with a bow and arrow which his father used for catching birds, and a small rucksack filled with basic supplies, Tjan made his way towards the rainforest. After a day of travel he had reached the outskirts. Here, amongst the increasingly dense mass of towering trees, there were trails leading inwards. Local people often wandered along these trails hunting small creatures and picking fruit .Tjan began to walk along these well worn paths. This part of the rainforest was relatively safe. As he walked, dead leaves crunched under his feet. Above him, monkeys scampered along the tree branches, staring at him in curiosity. Brightly coloured lizards darted everywhere. All around him was the constant hum of the rainforest insects interspersed with the sweet melodies of birds singing. Further and further Tjan walked, looking hopefully for the shiny, heart shaped, fluorescent green leaves that were characteristic of the Bawaka tree. However, he already knew that the likelihood of finding the leaf so quickly was remote. To have a chance of finding the leaf, he knew he would have to leave the safety of the trails.

Placing his hand in readiness, against the bow and arrow he carried at his side, Tjan began to move deeper into the rainforest. Constantly checking all around him for dangerous animals, he made his way through the trees and bushes. Tjan had some knowledge of the rainforest. And he knew that despite popular belief, the larger animals of the rainforest were rarely seen. Rainforest predators, such as tigers, panthers and leopards, preferred to do their hunting at night, and on the whole they avoided man, unless, they were very hungry. And despite the many stories of there being snakes in the jungle that could consume a whole man, there were only a few incidences where this had actually happened. On the whole, snakes preferred their victims unclothed.

Still, it was scary to know that despite the fact that he could not see these creatures, they were around. Perhaps they were lurking in the shadows. Perhaps they could see him. Suddenly Tjan heard a noise, in the bushes. He froze, petrified. Was it a tiger? A jaguar? A panther? He turned slowly and saw not an animal but a man. Tjan knew immediately that it was one of the rainforest people – a Qsari. The man's face was daubed with red paint and he wore a fierce expression. He stood poised with a bow and arrow ready to shoot.

What should Tjan do? Should he:

| Choice 1: Attack | Choice 2: Hide | Choice 3: Run |

| Choice 4: Approach |

Choice 1: Attack

Panicking, Tjan positioned his bow and fired an arrow wildly towards the man. The Qsari gave a wail of pain so loud it startled monkeys on the nearby tree branches who scampered off into the distance. And then Tjan heard the thud of the man fall. Tjan rushed towards the man dreading what he might find. At that moment he did not know whether he hoped that he had killed him – or hoped that he had not. Pushing the bushes aside he saw the Qsari man lying on the ground, staring at him with agonised eyes. The arrow was buried deep in his left hand side underneath his chest. But he was alive. Suddenly Tjan heard a flurry of movement, human voices, screams and shouts. Before he could grasp what was happening, he was surrounded by a group of men and women. All of their faces were daubed with stripes of red paint. The Qsari.

Tjan was grabbed roughly and dragged along by two short, stocky men. Finally, they reached a cleared area of the rainforest where there were a few large huts which had thatched roofs made of leaves supported by several tall timber logs. None of the huts had walls. Tjan realised that this was the Qsari settlement. Tjan found himself being harshly tied to a tree and he watched as the man that he'd shot was carried into the hut that was opposite. A young woman rushed forwards towards the injured man, screamed, and then began to cry loudly. The sound was heartbreaking. Was that the man's wife? His sister? Tjan closed his eyes and said a silent prayer – hoping that the man would be alright. Hoping that he would not die.

Suddenly Tjan heard a woman shout, "Bawaka! Bawaka!" and then two of the Qsari men rushed off disappearing into the thickness of the surrounding trees. Tjan stared after them but he could not see where they had gone.

Minutes later the men returned, carrying with them several large Bawaka tree leaves. Rushing into the house they began to press the leaves against the man's wound. For a few moments it seemed that everyone had forgotten about Tjan and then one of the older Qsari women came out of the hut and approached him.

"Why did you do this?" she asked softly.

"I'm sorry," Tjan replied nervously, "but I thought he was going to kill me."

"No..." the lady said gently. "The man you shot – his name is Talo. He was hunting for food."

"But he was pointing his arrow at me," Tjan explained.

"He would never use it," the woman replied quietly. "You scared him. That's all. But he would never shoot another human. That is not our way."

"I'm sorry," Tjan repeated.

The woman looked at him searchingly and then she nodded.

"I know," she said. And then she walked away.

Tjan watched the woman walk off and speak with one of the older Qsari men. Then they both turned and walked towards him.

"My name is Effiki and this is my husband Ajano. We are the village leaders," the woman explained to Tjan. "The man you shot is our son."

"Will he be OK?" Tjan asked.

"I'm not sure," the woman answered, her eyes filled with tears and then she averted her gaze.

The man stared at him for a few seconds, expressionless, and then stepping forward he walked behind Tjan and untied his arms.

"Go," the man said simply, "leave now."

Tjan looked at the two people standing in front of him not knowing what to say. Sorry did not seem enough. Finally, Tjan spoke saying the only thing he could think of:

"Thank you."

There were other words he wanted to say. Words that remained in his head. He wanted to say – Where is the Bawaka tree? Where is it? Can you just show me where? But he did not ask. How could he?

Tjan took one last glance behind him as he walked away. Effiki and Ajano had gone back into the hut to be close to their son. The woman he had seen screaming and crying was standing by Talo's bedside, weeping. No one was watching him as he left.

As Tjan made his way through the rainforest back towards his village, he listened carefully for the sounds of any approaching animals. And he looked around him, searching... hoping to see the Bawaka tree. But search as he might, he did not find it. He had failed – and not only that, he did not think that he would ever forget the agony in Talo's eyes. Or the faces of his parents. Eventually, Tjan found he had made his way back to the trails – and then following the trails out of the rainforest he headed home. As Tjan neared his village, he knew that he had already lost his father. And he knew that, because of his actions, a mother and father had almost lost their son.

TO KEEP A READING JOURNAL

Book Title/Author:

My First Impressions
Before beginning reading, look at the front cover. What genre is the book? Do you like the front cover? What do you like about it? Does the book look interesting? Does the cover make you want to read the book? Be honest.

Opening of the Story
Read a few pages then stop. Summarise what has happened so far. Are you enjoying the story? Predict what you think will happen next.

Story Development
Read up to half-way.
- Identify some of the events in the story. What is the most important thing that has happened?
- Describe the main characters using adjectives. Refer to the text. Give examples of things they have done and discuss their personalities.
- In most stories the main character has problems, dilemmas or conflicts. Write about some of the problems the main character faces.
- Identify and then describe some of the settings in the story.
- Look at the language in the story. Find examples of descriptive language and write them down.

Thoughts on the Ending
Read to the end of the book. What happened at the end of the story? Did you like the ending? Why or why not?

Reviewing the Story
- Think about some of the things that happened to the main character. Choose a part of the story where the main character felt happy, sad, excited or angry. Describe what happened.
- Express your opinion of the story. Did you like the story? What was the best part of the story? Are there any parts of the story you didn't like? Would you recommend the book to a friend?

Extension
- Write a letter to the author telling him/her what you thought about the book.
- Read another book by the same author.

CHANGES

Sacha barely took notice when she heard the phone ring. She was in the middle of reading her new Jacqueline Wilson book and it was just getting to the good bit. Then she heard her mum climbing up the stairs. She sat up as her mum opened the bedroom door and put the book on the bed beside her.

"Was it Dad?" Sacha asked.

"Yes it was," her mother answered. "He said to tell you that Lisa's had the baby. You've got a new sister."

Sacha's mum reached out and put her hand on Sacha's shoulder.

"How do you feel?" her mum asked gently.

"I'm alright," Sacha replied shrugging.

Her mum didn't look convinced. Sasha hoped her mum wouldn't ask her any more questions – because the truth was that she didn't want to talk about how she felt – because she wasn't sure. Part of her felt excited that she had a new sister. She immediately wondered what she looked like. But at the same time, another part of her wished that her new baby sister didn't exist. And she knew she could never tell anyone that. Because it was such a horrible thing to think. But she felt it all the same. Sacha looked closely at her mother. Surely this must be strange for her too.

"How do you feel Mum?" she asked.

Her mum looked surprised at the question. She frowned, thinking for a few seconds before answering.

"Well, it's been three years since me and your dad split up," her mum replied. "He's moved on and so have I."

Sacha's mum stood up.

"Your dad will be here in an hour," she explained. "He's going to take you to the hospital to see the new baby."

Her mum left the room leaving Sacha alone with her thoughts. Sacha sighed. Her dad had moved on and had a new girlfriend – and now a new baby. And only two weeks ago, her mum had introduced her to some man called Ian. Apparently, Ian was her mum's new friend. Sacha wondered how long it would take before her mum admitted the truth – that Ian was her new *boyfriend*. It seemed to Sacha that she was the only one finding it hard to move on. She wished that things would go back to the way they were before....

Of course it had been difficult to adjust after her dad had moved out. After countless arguments with her mum, he'd gone to stay with his brother – Uncle Peter. Sacha had spent the first six months desperately hoping that her mum and dad would get back together. But then her dad had announced he was buying a new house. And Sacha had known what that meant. Why would her dad buy a new house if he was planning on moving back in with her and her mum? She'd realised he was never coming back. Finally, a few months later the divorce had come through. And that was that. Her mum and dad were no longer married.

Sasha had had to get used to mainly seeing her dad at the weekends. She had her own bedroom at her dad's house and she'd made friends with the girl who lived next door. Her name was Gemma and she was the same age. After a while Sacha had stopped dreaming of her mum and dad getting back together. What was the point? It wasn't going to happen. And Sacha realised something. She didn't miss listening to the arguments. She didn't miss the nights when she'd lay in bed trying to blank out the sound of her mum and dad shouting at each other. She didn't want to go back to that.

So Sacha had got used to her new life. She looked forward to going down to her dad's. They had fun together. Just her and her dad. Quite often he'd take her shopping and buy her new things. He'd always say yes when she asked if they could stop off at McDonald's. Sometimes he'd take her and her friend Gemma to Wacky Warehouse or the park. Every Saturday night they'd choose a video to watch together. But best of all were the long talks she had found herself having with her dad. She would tell him all about school, friends and what had happened in the week. And he seemed to have a lot more time to listen than he had before. When her parents split up everything had changed but Sacha had got used to it. She was happy with the way things were. Until just over a year ago, when things had began to change – again.

She'd gone round to her dad's one weekend and he'd introduced her to his new friend Lisa. Lisa seemed OK. She was friendly and chatted with Sacha asking her lots of questions about school. Sacha had made sure she was polite to Lisa. She didn't want to be rude to one of her dad's friends. But the truth was that Sacha had felt a bit irritated. She was used to having her dad all to herself at the weekends. She wondered why Lisa was there. The following weekend Lisa was there again. After that, it seemed like every time she went round to her dad's house Lisa was there. When Lisa began to stay late on a Saturday to cook dinner and watch videos with them, Sacha realised what was going on. She'd already guessed before her dad finally told her – Lisa was his new *girlfriend*.

A few months later, Lisa had moved in. And then, before Sacha had even had time to get used to that, her dad had told her that he and Lisa were having a baby. It'd been hard enough to get used to sharing her dad with Lisa. She wondered if her dad would have any time for her at all, now that he had a new baby....

Sacha's thoughts were interrupted by the sound of a car horn bipping. And then her mum shouted up the stairs:

"Sacha – your dad's here!"

Sacha stood up and took a deep breath. She decided that she wasn't going to act all childish and jealous. She was ten years old – too old to act like that. And even if she did feel a bit upset it wasn't the new baby's fault. She walked out to the car and smiled when she saw her dad sitting in the driver's seat.

"Hi Dad," she said. "Congratulations!"

"Thanks," her dad replied looking pleased.

As they drove to the hospital her dad filled her in with some of the details. The baby had been born a few hours ago. She had curly black hair and huge eyes. She was six pounds two ounces which was tiny. He and Lisa had decided to call the baby Amélie.

They arrived at the hospital and her dad parked the car, then he looked over at

Sacha.

"How do you feel – about the new baby?" he asked.

"Mum asked me that. I'm fine," Sacha replied nonchalantly.

Sacha could tell by looking at her dad's face that he didn't believe her.

"OK," Sacha admitted, "it's just that there have been so many changes. First you and Mum split up. Now, I have to get used to a new sister. I don't know. I feel a bit confused. Everything changes all the time. Nothing stays the same. "

Her dad didn't answer straight away. There was a few seconds of silence as though he was thinking about what to say. Then he smiled.

"Things do change Sacha," he explained gently. "That's part of life. I remember when you were just a baby – just as small as Amélie. And now you'll soon be starting secondary school. You've changed. You're smart, you're sensible – and you're going to make a brilliant big sister."

Sacha thought about the idea of being a big sister and realised she liked it. She would be able to help take care of Amélie – look after her, give her advice – that sort of thing. Suddenly, she didn't feel so confused anymore. She was really looking forward to meeting her new sister.

"Honestly Dad – I feel OK!" Sacha said smiling. And this time she meant it. "Let's go and see Amélie!"

DUPPY ISLAND

Oliver slowly opened his eyes. At first, he saw a mist of hazy blue interspersed with sharp glints of light. As his surroundings came into focus, he realised he was staring upwards, into the brightness of the shimmering sun in an azure sky. Oliver felt the soft warmth of the sand against his body. Soon, he became aware of a persistent splash of water against his feet.

Carefully Oliver manoeuvred himself into a sitting position. He realised that his feet were half in the sea and soft waves were gently lapping against his toes. His head felt fuzzy with pain. Gingerly, he touched his brow and removing his hand he looked down at his fingers. Blood. His throat felt parched and dry. Running his tongue over his lips he tasted the acrid saltiness of the sea. Suddenly, he felt desperately thirsty.

Slowly, Oliver looked around him. The view that he saw was so staggeringly beautiful it belonged on a picture postcard. There was an abundance of palm trees heavy with coconuts scattered across a white sandy beach. In front of him, the turquoise blue sea sparkled so brilliantly it seemed as if diamonds floated on its surface. Towards the left of the island there was a tangle of lush green vegetation. There was nothing scary about his surroundings, but despite this, Oliver felt a growing sense of unease.

With every second that passed, Oliver's head became clearer. Suddenly he had a flash of memory – a vivid image of himself struggling to cling to a piece of wood; huge waves whipping his body from side to side, throwing him against the jagged edges of rocks. Oliver's sense of fear increased as he realised where he was. He was in a place that no one wanted to be. A place no one ever visited despite its stunning beauty. He was on Duppy Island.

* * * * * * * * *

For the past three years, Oliver had spent two weeks of the six week school holiday visiting his Uncle Jim and Aunty Dorothy at their home situated close to the beach on the island of St Levy's. The day had started out like so many other days on the island. The weather had been blisteringly hot. The sea was calm and peaceful. It was a perfect day for sailing. At around lunchtime, Uncle Jim had suggested they go and catch some fish for their evening meal. The last time they had been fishing, Aunty Dorothy had washed and cleaned up the fish, seasoned it with delicious spices, and then fried it, serving it up with sweet tasting dumplings. Oliver's mouth had begun watering almost immediately at the thought. He could hardly wait. As Uncle Jim and Oliver set sail, Oliver considered how lucky he was to have an aunt and uncle who lived in what many people would view as a tropical paradise.

Uncle Jim had told him how the waters of the Caribbean contained hundreds of tiny, unexplored, uninhabited islands. Each time they sailed they would pass a particular small island that was a few miles away from St Levy's. Oliver had questioned his Uncle

Jim about it. When his uncle had explained that it was a desert island, Oliver had been filled with excitement. Fascinated with the idea of exploring a real life desert island he had begged his uncle to take him there. But Uncle Jim had refused point blank, insisting that it was far too dangerous. He had explained to Oliver that close to the island there were jagged rocks beneath the surface of the sea. Although they could not be seen from a distance, these rocks surrounded the island and they would pierce the underside of any vessel that went near, causing serious damage. And then Uncle Jim had explained that there was another reason no one had ever tried to go to the island.

"The island is known by everyone as Duppy Island," Uncle Jim had told him.

On hearing this, Oliver had laughed. He knew that the word 'duppy' was a Caribbean word meaning "malevolent ghost or spirit". He couldn't believe that Uncle Jim believed in such things. But his laughter faded when he saw the sombre expression on his uncle's face.

"I'm serious," Uncle Jim continued. "It's no joking matter. No one who has even got close to that island has lived to tell the tale."

Uncle Jim explained how two hundred years ago, the island of St Levy's had been filled with slave plantations. The slaves had been people who were captured in Africa and then brought over to the island by ship. On arrival, they had been forced to work in the sizzling hot sun, chopping sugar cane to produce sugar, which was then sold to other countries. The slaves had been strictly guarded. Any slaves who refused to work were beaten by the masters of the plantations; punishments were severe for any slave who tried to escape. Oliver had learnt about slavery in school. The idea of it made him sad. He hated to imagine what it would be like to be treated so brutally and to have no hope of freedom from such a terrible life.

"Many tried to escape but few could," Uncle Jim explained. "But there is a legend about one of the brave people who managed to get away. His name was Phileus Johnson."

Oliver had listened as Uncle Jim had told him how Phileus had gained his freedom. Phileus had been a slave on a plantation not far from the sea. After managing to escape, Phileus had run down to the shore angrily followed by his pursuers. Diving into the sea, he had managed to swim from St Levy's to the place now known as Duppy Island. No one knows how he managed to swim so far. At first the plantation owners assumed he had drowned. But then there had been several sightings of a man matching Phileus' description on the small desert island.

The plantation owners had been furious that Phileus had escaped their clutches. Desperate to capture him, they mounted several bids to get to the small island. All were unsuccessful. Each time, one of two things would happen, boats approaching the island would get caught on the jagged rocks and overturn drowning the occupants, or anyone who actually managed to navigate their way through the rocks and set foot on the island would be greeted by Phileus shooting poisonous arrows at them. These arrows would instantly kill. After six men lost their lives trying to get Phileus, they decided the cost of retrieving one slave was too great and they let him be. It must have been a lonely life for Phileus, living on the island by himself. But it seemed he preferred to live his life alone and free rather than return to a life of slavery.

Phileus lived and died on the island. Local superstition believed that even though this all took place over two hundred years ago, the ghost of Phileus still remained there – which is why it was known as Duppy Island. It was thought that anyone who went close to the island would meet their deaths on the rocks or if they managed to reach the shore, they would be killed by one of Phileus' poisonous arrows.

So earlier that day, when without warning the sky had suddenly darkened and a fierce storm had developed, Uncle Jim had tried desperately to steer the boat away from the only land they were close to, Duppy Island. Uncle Jim had radioed for help and then tried desperately to gain control of the vessel. But the violent winds had relentlessly pushed against the small boat blowing them towards the island and its treacherous rocks. There had been an ear-splitting crunch as the sharp point of one of the rocks had torn into the underside of the boat, splintering the timber. Then the boat had capsized. Oliver remembered Uncle Jim pushing him a floating piece of wood and shouting, "Hang on!" Oliver had grabbed it. Then the strong current in the water had pushed Oliver towards the rocks. Pushing him closer to the island. And that was all he remembered. Until he opened his eyes and found he was lying in the sand.

* * * * * * * * * *

Oliver tried to stand up but a wave of dizziness meant that he had to sit down again immediately.

Well, I'm still alive, Oliver thought to himself. At least I haven't been killed by a poisonous arrow.

And then he heard a noise like the cracking of a twig. His heart began to beat faster and he turned his head towards the sound. It came from the left of the beach where there was a thick tangle of green bushes. Then he heard it again. Something... or someone was in there. Phileus, thought Oliver struggling to his feet, Phileus had come for him. He took a few steps and then collapsed into the sand. Oliver felt as if he was in the middle of dreams he'd had where some unknown terror came closer and he found he couldn't speak or move properly. He wanted to beg Phileus not to shoot him. To explain to him that no one was coming to hurt him, to capture him or to take him back to the plantation. He wanted to tell him that it was a different time; a different century and that slavery didn't exist anymore. But Oliver felt paralysed with fear and no words came out. He could only sit in the sand watching as the shadowy outline of a man appeared in the bushes. Finally, the man pushed the bushes aside and stepped through them walking towards Oliver. And to Oliver's relief he recognised him.

"Uncle Jim!" smiled Oliver finding his voice at last.

Uncle Jim had managed to swim to another part of the island and as soon as he had reached the shore he had began searching for Oliver. Thankfully, it didn't take long for help to arrive. The coastguard had been able to identify the location from Uncle Jim's radio message and sent a helicopter to the island. Luckily for Oliver, his head injury wasn't serious – just a superficial graze. But with the combination of suffering from the beginnings of heatstroke and dehydration, Oliver had been slightly delirious and incredibly weak. Which explained why he'd found it so difficult to stand. After lots of water and a few days' rest, Oliver was fine.

In later years, Oliver would sometimes find himself thinking about the sad story of the runaway slave who had lived and died on the island. He wondered whether the ghost of Phileus really existed. And if so – why hadn't he tried to hurt Oliver and Uncle Jim? Oliver realised he would never know the answers to these questions but he hoped that Phileus was now resting in peace.

WHY WAS GANDHI IMPORTANT?

Mohandas Karamchand Gandhi was born in 1869 in India. As a boy he was shy and reserved. No one could have guessed that he would grow up to become one of the most important leaders of all time.

At the time of Gandhi's birth, India was ruled by the British. As was tradition, Gandhi married young (he and his bride Kasturbai were only thirteen). Later, Gandhi decided he wanted to be a lawyer. When he was eighteen he went to study in England. After he had completed his studies he returned to India for a while before taking up a job opportunity in South Africa.

While he was there he realised that the Indian people living in South Africa were treated very badly. He experienced this first hand when he was thrown off a train because he was in the wrong compartment. He had sat in first class but this was not allowed. The laws in South Africa at that time stated that all dark skinned people were meant to travel third class. Gandhi decided that this was unfair and that he would try to do something about it.

Gandhi began to speak out against racial injustice. He encouraged other Indians to refuse to follow unfair laws. However, despite the fact that Gandhi had decided he wanted to make a stand against the government, he was a man of peace. He urged his followers not to fight with 'guns and swords' but to use non-violent methods to protest.

Indians who refused to follow the laws were punished. Hundreds of Indians were arrested and some died. Gandhi himself was arrested on several occasions. But however badly he was treated, he did not fight back. Gradually, he began to achieve respect and this led to changes in some of the laws.

Gandhi returned to India in 1915 when he was forty-five years old. India was still ruled by the British at this time, and some of the laws enforced by the British were unfair to Indian people. Unsurprisingly, many Indians did not want Britain to rule India. In 1919, a crowd of Indian people met up in the square in the town of Amristar. The British soldiers were ordered to shoot at the crowd to disperse them. 379 Indian people were killed and over 1,200 injured.

This event was one of the saddest days in the history of India. Gandhi decided that the actions of the British soldiers were unacceptable and agreed that the time had come for the British to leave India. However, following the same principles as he had done in South Africa, he decided to protest against British rule in a peaceful way.

It took many years for change to come about and Gandhi was arrested several times. In 1930 Gandhi organised one of his most famous protests commonly referred to as 'The Salt March'. The British had made a law which meant that anyone who needed salt had to buy it from the government and pay a high tax. This was an unfair law because everyone needed to buy salt but it was hard for poor people to pay the tax. Worst of all, it was easy enough to get salt from the sea – but this was not allowed.

During the The Salt March, Gandhi and thousands of his followers marched down to a place by the sea where the salt lay on the beach. Gandhi picked up a handful and so did his followers. The government was furious. Soon many of the poor people all over India copied Gandhi and began producing their own salt. At least 60,000 people were arrested and as the disobedience spread, Gandhi was once more thrown into prison.

The protests continued. On one occasion, more than 2,000 people who had marched down to the Dharasana salt works to protest were attacked and beaten by police and soldiers. Despite provocation, they followed Gandhi's instructions and did not retaliate. An American journalist witnessed this event and the British were embarrassed when newspaper reports were published describing how the Indians had refused to fight back in the face of such brutality.

Gandhi was now recognised as a powerful force and in 1931 he was invited to Britain to discuss the future of India. However, it was to be a while longer before India was released from British rule. On his return to India, Gandhi continued quietly protesting and as a result spent much of his time in jail. His wife Kasturbai was also arrested and sadly she died in his arms in prison in 1944.

At last in 1947, India was set free from British rule. There were great celebrations; however, there were still problems in India. Because people of different religions kept fighting each other, the country was split into two – Hindu India and Muslim Pakistan. Gandhi was a Hindu but he respected people of different religions and wanted everyone to live together peacefully. The fighting between people of the two religions became worse and Gandhi decided to fast, to show how much he disagreed with it. In response to his fast the fighting calmed and agreements were made between religious leaders.

However, despite these agreements some Hindus and Muslims did not like Gandhi. They did not agree with his idea that people of different religions should live in peace. In 1948, a Hindu extremist took Gandhi's life firing three bullets at him during a prayer meeting. Gandhi cried, "Hai Rama!" (which means "Oh God") before falling to the ground.

Gandhi was prepared to die for what he believed. He showed it was possible to bring about change through non-violent protest. His teachings have inspired many other influential leaders including the famous civil rights leader, Martin Luther King.

SIGNIFICANT DATES IN THE LIFE OF MAHATMA GANDHI

1869 – Mohandas Karamchand Gandhi was born in Porbander, India.

1883 – Marries Kasturbai Makhanji – they are both thirteen years old.

1888 – Leaves India to go to England to study law.

1891 – Qualifies as a lawyer and then returns to India.

1893 – Leaves India to go to South Africa to work as a lawyer.

1915 – Returns to India – he is forty-five years old.

1919 – 379 people killed and 1,200 injured in the massacre at Amritsar.

1930 – 'The Salt March' takes place.

1931 – Gandhi goes to England to meet with British officials to discuss the future of India.

1944 – Gandhi's wife Kasturbai dies in prison.

1947 – India is released from British rule and divided into two separate countries – India and Pakistan.

1948 – On the 30th of January, Gandhi is shot dead by a Hindu extremist.

AMRITSAR: AN IMAGINARY AUTOBIOGRAPHICAL ACCOUNT

In 1919 a crowd of Indian people met up in the town of Amritsar. At this time India was ruled by the British. The British soldiers were ordered to shoot at the crowd to disperse them. 379 Indian people were killed and over 1,200 injured. People around the world, including many British people, were shocked and saddened by what happened. Below is an imaginary, autobiographical account of someone who was part of the incident.

On the day of the massacre a great number of people had gathered in Jallianwala Bagh, Amritsar. We wished to show our support for Gandhi and also, it was the Sikh Festival 'Baisakhi Fair'. Everything was peaceful even though there were over 3,000 of us.

We listened as people spoke of how they had been badly treated by the British Army. The British Army Commander was very cruel. His name was General Dyer. Stories of how he had instructed his soldiers to do horrible things to our people made me angry. An old man spoke of how he had been made to crawl along the street on his hands and knees. Another man described how he had been whipped. Under General Dyers' orders the people of our country had been humiliated and degraded.

I am sure that other members of the crowd felt as angry as me. But we were not there to fight. Ghandi had told us 'We must never fight back even if we have to die to set our country free'. So we listened calmly, unaware that in the minutes ahead, just as Gandhi had predicted, many of us would die.

The gun fire started without warning. Suddenly, for no reason at all, General Dyer ordered the British troops to begin firing into the crowd. Some people fell immediately. The air was filled with the sound of screams as the remaining people scattered, panicking, running this way and that – trying to escape the bullets.

Instinctively I dived to the ground. A young man of about twenty, lay on the floor beside me – dead. I heard the sound of someone whimpering in pain but I dared not turn my head to see who it was. I was too scared to move. It seemed that the gun fire would never end. I heard later that the troops fired continuously for fifteen minutes.

After the shooting had stopped I lay there for a long time, still afraid. Then, when I was sure the soldiers had gone, I stood up and looked around me. I will never forget what I saw. The ground was littered with bodies and blood. Injured people wailed and begged for help.

I survived the massacre of Amritsar – but the memories of that terrible day will be with me forever.

CITY CHILDREN ARRIVE IN LINLEY HAYES

Evacuees sent from the nearby city of Birmingham arrived in the village of Linley Hayes at around 2.00 p.m. on 24th September, 1939. Residents of Linley Hayes have been asked to open their hearts and their homes to welcome the children from the big city. The children have been sent to various locations in the countryside as there is a real danger of houses in built-up city areas being bombed by the Germans.

After arriving at the train station, the children were taken to the village hall and lined up. Following this, the local residents selected the children they wished to take home. The older, healthy looking boys were among the first to be chosen. This is probably due to the fact that many of the residents of Linley Hayes have farms and feel that the boys will be able to help them out. Also popular were girls aged nine years old and above whom residents felt could be a big help around the house.

Any villagers with enough space in their homes were expected to take in the evacuees. Most were keen to do their part to support the war against the Germans and were excited about receiving their new guests. Mrs Eileen Milford said:

"I love children. I have two grown up sons who are away fighting in the war, whom I miss very much. My husband and I are looking forward to having children around the house again. They can learn all about the animals on the farm!"

Although most residents were enthusiastic, a few expressed reservations. Mrs Evelyn Stauton commented:

"Of course I'll do whatever it takes to support the war. My husband and I live in a two bedroom house and we have a spare room so we have to take at least one child. However, the truth is that I don't really like children. But as long as they're quiet and do as they're told there won't be a problem."

The majority of evacuees were relocated within two hours of arrival. Unfortunately, at the present time there are still three children who haven't been chosen by any of the villagers. These children have had no choice but to spend the night sleeping on the floor of the village hall. It is unclear what is going to happen to the unwanted children. However, because of the dangers of living in the big city, it is unlikely that they will be sent back to Birmingham. All the residents are urged to consider very carefully whether they could find any additional space at all in their homes to provide a place of safety for the remaining evacuees.

Reported by Leon Hughes.

EVACUEE INTERVIEW

Geraldine Harlow is an evacuee who has been sent from the City of Birmingham to live in the village of Linley Hayes. She was unlucky enough to be one of the children who were not selected by any of the prospective foster parents on the first night. Poor Geraldine spent her first night in Linley Hayes sleeping on the floor of the church hall. However, the following day, Mrs Ida Henshaw, a widower, came forward and offered to take care of her. I spoke to Geraldine to find out how she is adapting to life in Linley Hayes.

How long have you been in the village Geraldine?
Nearly four weeks now.

Do you like living with Mrs Henshaw?
Yes I do. She's a kind lady. I felt really sad when no one picked me on the first day. I was glad when she came the next day and said she would take me home.

Why do you think no one chose you?
I don't know why. It was horrible standing there waiting to be picked. I was crying on that first night when I had to sleep on the floor of the village hall.

How do you feel now? Are you happy?
I still cry sometimes when I think about my mum and dad. My dad's away fighting in the war and my mum's in Birmingham. Sometimes I feel lonely.

Is life in the countryside different from life in the city?
Yes, it really is. Before I came to the countryside I'd never seen a real cow or a sheep. I'd only seen them in books. I like the animals and also the countryside is much prettier than Birmingham – there are lots of trees, flowers and fields everywhere instead of just houses.

What is Mrs Henshaw's house like?
It's a small cottage with a huge garden. There are apple trees in the garden which is great because I love apples. It's not a farm but Mrs Henshaw keeps chickens. I help look after the chickens and collect the eggs.

Some evacuees have complained that they have to do lots of work helping out on the farms or in the house. Has this happened to you?
Well I do a lot of the housework but I don't mind. Mrs Henshaw is very old – she's seventy-four. She has a bad back and it's hard for her to keep the house clean so I like helping her. I'm good at doing housework – I always used to help my mum.

Do you get any time to play?

Yes, lots. Another evacuee called Peter lives not far away. After I've finished the housework, I meet up with him and we run about in the fields and play different games like hide-and-seek or climb trees.

So it's not all bad then?

It's not bad at all. It's like a holiday really. But even though I like it, I want to go home. I miss living in Birmingham and I miss my mum.

RADIO NEWS BULLETIN: THE BIRMINGHAM BLITZ

This is Connor Grantham with today's news.

This morning parts of Birmingham have been reduced to rubble following a night of heavy bombing by the Germans. Residents described hearing the sound of approaching aircraft before the bombs started to fall. Sirens warned residents to take cover and many people spent the night in air raid shelters or in the safest part of their homes – underneath the staircase.

Several people who received injuries in the air raid have been taken to hospitals in the local area. As yet the number of fatalities is unknown. There are still several members of the public who are unaccounted for.

It is thought that the intention of the air raids was to cripple the transport system by blowing up roads. Many houses and pubs were destroyed during the bombings, and Birmingham city centre suffered heavy damage. The Bull Ring shopping area was targeted and the market hall was almost completed destroyed.

As a result of the bombing, there are still areas of the city that are on fire. The blazes are being tackled by Birmingham Fire Service. Many roads around the city centre are blocked. However, despite the efforts of the Germans, buses are still running today although there is a reduced service. The public are advised not to travel unless it is absolutely necessary.

Officials have stated that it is highly likely that the bombing will resume tonight. Reports indicate that nightly air raids on Birmingham are set to continue for the foreseeable future. Residents are being advised to leave their homes and seek alternative accommodation in a safer location if possible. However, many residents say they have nowhere else to go. Other people are refusing to leave their homes, seeing this as a sign of giving in to the Germans.

SHOULD ANIMALS BE ALLOWED TO PERFORM IN CIRCUSES?

For	Against
• It is entertaining to watch animals performing tricks.	• It is degrading for animals to be forced to perform tricks for human entertainment.
• Most people expect to see animals when they come to the circus.	• Animals are not needed as people prefer watching other acts such as the trapeze artist.
• The circus owners provide homes for the animals.	• Animals like lions are kept in small cages which is not fair.
• Circus owners provide food and regular exercise for the animals.	• Some circus owners do not look after the animals properly.
• The animals like performing.	• The animals may not like performing but have no choice.
• Circuses provide an opportunity for people to see wild animals.	• Animals should be left in the wild where they belong.

I believe that it is fine for some animals like horses to be used in circuses if the circus owners look after them and take them out for rides. However, I feel it is quite wrong for animals like lions to be kept in small cages and to have to perform silly tricks. In my opinion wild animals should not be used in circuses.

SHOULD PRIMARY SCHOOL PUPILS BE ALLOWED TO BRING MOBILE PHONES TO SCHOOL?

Most adults own mobile phones and view them as a necessity which enables them to cope with their busy lifestyles. Increasingly, parents are buying mobile phones for their children. Teachers have noted that children as young as six have begun bringing their mobile phones to school. The issue has sparked debate among parents, teachers and pupils over whether it is necessary for children to bring their mobile phones to school.

Parents cite several reasons for giving their children mobile phones. The most common reason is that they are concerned about their children's safety when travelling to and from school. They believe that with a mobile phone their children can call them at any time if they have a problem. In addition, some parents feel that mobile phones are useful on occasions when they need to discuss after school arrangements with their child. A further reason mentioned by a few of the children is that many of their friends have the latest mobile phones and they don't want to be left out.

On the other hand, many teachers express the view that most primary school pupils do not need to bring mobile phones to school. The opinion of most teachers is that if parents need to contact their children for some reason during school hours, then they can always phone the school secretary. Some teachers believe that the main reason children bring mobile phones to school is simply to show off to their friends. However, teachers do understand the benefits for an older child, who has to travel a long distance on their own, carrying a phone for safety reasons. In addition, teachers agree that mobiles can be useful for older children who need to contact their parents after school. However, in cases such as these, teachers feel that mobile phones should be left in the school office and that children should not be allowed to have them during lesson time – and most pupils and parents agreed with this.

In conclusion, it seems that most parents, teachers and children do not feel it is necessary for the majority of primary aged pupils to bring mobile phones to school with them. However, it is agreed that there are exceptions and on occasion (such as if an older child needs to make arrangements with their parents after school) mobiles can be useful. It is interesting to note that, despite the fact that there is a general consensus that most primary school children do not need to bring mobile phones to school – more and more children are bringing them!

THE IMPORTANCE OF HEALTHY EATING

There is a growing concern that many children would prefer to eat junk food rather than eat a healthy diet. If children are asked what their favourite foods are, many will mention chips, biscuits, cakes and burgers. Very few will say fresh fruit and vegetables. Often parents and teachers set a bad example by frequently indulging in unhealthy food themselves! It is important to remember the many reasons why eating healthily is good for us.

Firstly, if we eat the right foods the benefits are immediate. We soon feel more energetic and able to concentrate. For example, there is a huge difference in the energy levels of a child who has had a good healthy breakfast and one who has not. It is likely that children who regularly have a filling breakfast, such as wholegrain cereals and toast, will do much better at school than those who do not.

Secondly, eating healthy foods helps make us stronger and less prone to illness. There are many different essential vitamins and minerals to be found in fruit and vegetables which build our resistance to disease. Research shows that people who eat healthy foods like fruit, vegetables and fish tend to live longer. On the other hand, continually eating fatty or sugary foods can lead to serious problems like obesity and heart disease.

Thirdly, eating unhealthy food is a waste of valuable time. Foods like cakes and sweets have limited nutritional value. Although these foods do fill you up momentarily and supply you with a short burst of energy, this doesn't last long. Consequently, you will probably feel hungry again shortly after eating them. In addition, sugary foods are extremely bad for your teeth!

Finally, a great reason for eating healthy food is that it tastes good. There are a huge range of delicious tasting fruits and vegetables to choose from. And most people would agree a nutritious home cooked meal tastes wonderful.

In conclusion it is vitally important that we remind ourselves of the many reasons there are to eat healthily. Children who eat well are likely to feel more energetic, do better at school and ultimately they will probably live longer too.

A GUIDE TO TRENT HILL PRIMARY SCHOOL

General Information

Trent Hill Junior and Infant School is located in a busy city area in the North West of Dorley Town. There are 230 children on roll and one class per year group. The school is divided into three separate buildings – the Early Years Centre, the Infants and the Juniors.

The Early Years Centre

The Early Years Centre has an open plan design, enabling the children to freely explore their environment. The centre is organised into different areas linked to the curriculum. There is a maths area, a literacy area, and a science area. There are also areas where the children can learn through play such as the wet area containing the sand and water trays, the pretend shop and café and the role-play area, which has a selection of dressing up clothes. Displays are bright and interactive in order to stimulate the children's imagination.

The Infant Building

The infant building contains the Years 1 and 2 classrooms. Both of the classrooms are fairly spacious with walls painted in soothing pastel shades in order to promote a calm atmosphere. Classroom displays are of a high standard showing outstanding examples of the children's work. Both classrooms have an interactive whiteboard. Each classroom has two desktop computers which the children use to enhance their learning throughout the day. Infant classrooms have a reading area, a listening centre and an Art area. There is a small hall situated on the lower floor of the building which is used for P.E. lessons, assemblies and dinner times.

* Please note that infant classes visit the junior building for ICT, music and library sessions each week.

The Junior Building

The junior building contains the Years 3, 4, 5 and 6 classrooms. All of the junior classrooms have interactive whiteboards and two desktop computers. Each classroom is large, well decorated (in colours suggested by the children) with excellent classroom displays. This building contains the main school hall. Juniors use the hall for P.E., dinner time and assemblies. The hall is used for whole school assemblies twice a week. The school has a music room which contains a range of instruments. All children have lessons once a week from a specialist music teacher. The ICT suite in the junior building contains enough computers for every child in the class to be able to work individually. All of the ICT equipment is regularly updated. The school library is also located in the junior building. Classes visit the library once a week.

Outdoor Areas

The Early Years Centre has an excellent outside area with a wide range of nursery play equipment. There is a garden area for quiet play. One area of the garden is used for growing vegetables. Both infants and juniors have large playgrounds which contain climbing frames for the children to use at break times. In addition there are quiet areas where the children can go to sit quietly and relax. There is a small field adjacent to the playground area which is used for football and athletics.

If you are interested in sending your child to Trent Hill Primary School please call the school office on 111 - 4562 to arrange an interview with Mrs McKenroy the Headteacher.

A VISITOR'S GUIDE TO BLACKPOOL

Blackpool is the most popular tourist destination in the United Kingdom. There's something for everyone in Blackpool!

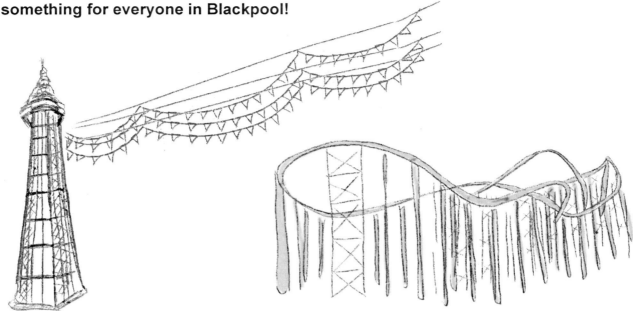

The Pleasure Beach

The Pleasure Beach is one of the most popular attractions in Blackpool. This amazing theme park has over 125 rides to choose from. The Pleasure Beach is suitable for all the family.

Blackpool Tower

The tower is 518 feet tall. Inside the tower there is a range of attractions such as the Tower Circus and the famous Tower Ballroom.

Blackpool Zoo

The zoo contains 1,500 animals from all over the world. It is divided into a number of different areas including Gorilla Mountain, Lemur Wood and Amazonia.

Louis Tussaud's Waxworks

The waxworks can be found opposite the Central Pier. Visitors can view hundreds of models including a range of famous celebrities.

Sandcastle Water Park

The water park is opposite the pleasure beach. It has over eighteen slides and attractions. The park is the largest water park in the United Kingdom.

Shopping

There are two main shopping areas. The town centre contains all of the well-known high street stores. There are numerous cafés, bars and benches dotted around and most of the area is pedestrianised. The Waterloo Road/Bond Street area in the south shore has lots of small, interesting shops. It is the ideal place to buy souvenirs.

Blackpool Illuminations

This dazzling display of lights is a huge tourist attraction. The illuminations are over ten kilometres long and use over one million bulbs.

Blackpool Beach

Let's not forget one of the most important attractions of all – the beach. Blackpool has a beautiful sandy beach which stretches for miles. The family can enjoy traditional beach activities like, swimming, building a sandcastle, relaxing in a deckchair and riding a donkey!

SUCCESS CRITERIA 12:
TO WRITE A HORROR STORY

- Centre your story around one main character so that the reader can identify with them.

- Keep the plot simple – but bring it to life with great description.

- Begin the story in a normal everyday setting.

- In the middle of the story move to a spookier setting. Use lots of adjectives to describe the setting.

- Introduce the scary characters slowly to build the tension, e.g. He heard a rustle in the bushes – what was it?

- Describe exactly what the scary character looks like so the reader can imagine it for themselves.

- Don't reveal everything at once – the reader should wonder what will happen.

- Describe how scared the main character feels. Try:
  - Using adjectives like terrified, afraid, worried etc.
  - Using adverbs like desperately, frantically, nervously etc.
  - Using descriptive phrases like – his legs shook, her heart pounded etc.

- Use a mix of shorter sentences and complex sentences.

- Include a range of punctuation.

- Think about how to end your story – a scary story can have lots of different endings – happy, sad, a cliff-hanger, a twist etc.

SELF/PEER ASSESSMENT SHEET 12:
TO WRITE A HORROR STORY

- [ ] Does the story centre around one main character?

- [ ] Is the plot fairly simple?

- [ ] Does the story start in a normal everyday setting?

- [ ] Is the spooky setting described well using lots of adjectives?

- [ ] Are any scary story characters introduced slowly to build the tension?

- [ ] Are any scary characters described well so that the reader can imagine what they look like?

- [ ] Are lots of adjectives and adverbs used to try to show how scared the main character feels? e.g. terrified, frantically...

- [ ] Does the story contain a mix of short sentences and longer complex sentences?

- [ ] Does the story include a range of punctuation?

- [ ] Does the story have a good ending?

How could this work be improved?

_____

_____

_____

_____

_____

_____

SUCCESS CRITERIA 13:
TO WRITE A SCIENCE FICTION STORY

- Set the story in the future.

- Organise the plot around the question 'What if...'. For example, What if aliens were to come to earth? What if robots took over the world? What if a meteor hit the planet? etc.

- Include a science fiction setting, e.g. another planet, the world fifty years into the future.

- Include unusual characters like strange aliens or robots or a main character who is a hero.

- Include lots of adjectives and descriptive phrases.

- Use short sentences and complex sentences.

- Write in paragraphs.

- Use a range of punctuation, e.g. capitals, full stops, commas, hyphens, ellipsis (...).

- The story should have a problem and a resolution at the end.

SELF/PEER ASSESSMENT SHEET 13:
TO WRITE A SCIENCE FICTION STORY

☐ Is the story set in the future?

☐ Is the plot based around a 'What if...?' question? For example, what if we found life on other planets?

☐ Does the story include a science fiction setting? For example, another planet, a spaceship, a future world.

☐ Does the story include science fiction characters (such as aliens) or a brave hero?

☐ Are there lots of adjectives and descriptive phrases in the story?

☐ Does the story include short sentences and longer complex sentences?

☐ Is the story written in paragraphs?

☐ Does the story have a range of punctuation? For example, capitals, full stops, commas, hyphens, ellipsis (...).

☐ Does the story have a problem?

☐ Is this problem resolved at the end?

How could this work be improved?

_____

_____

_____

_____

SUCCESS CRITERIA 14:
TO WRITE A HISTORICAL RECOUNT

- Write in first person – as though you are the main character, using the word 'I'.

- Try to sound as if you are talking or thinking aloud.

- Write events in the order in which they occurred.*

- Include details that show the recount is set in the past, e.g. jobs, events, items, settings and characters should be linked to the era you are writing about.

- Use a variety of sentence openers – don't keep using the word 'I' to begin every sentence.

- Use some sequencing words or phrases to help your writing flow, e.g. the next day, moments later, that afternoon, meanwhile, seconds later, suddenly.

- Use paragraphs.

- Include vivid descriptions to try to 'transport' the reader to the era you are describing.

- Describe your feelings and emotions using adjectives, adverbs and descriptive phrases.

- End with a good closing line – perhaps you could comment on how you are feeling about your life/events that have occurred.

* If appropriate, begin with a short introductory paragraph explaining what the recount will be about.

SELF/PEER ASSESSMENT SHEET 14:
TO WRITE A HISTORICAL RECOUNT

☐   Is the story written in first person?

☐   Does the recount contain details that show it is set in the past? e.g. jobs, events, items, settings and characters from the past.

☐   Are a variety of sentence openers used rather than continually beginning sentences with 'I'?

☐   Are sequencing words used? e.g. the next day, after that, in the afternoon etc.

☐   Are paragraphs used?

☐   Are the feelings of the main character described?

☐   Are lots of adjectives, adverbs and descriptive phrases used?

☐   Does the recount end with a good closing line? Perhaps commenting on how the main character is feeling about their life/events that have occurred.

How could this work be improved?

_____

_____

_____

_____

_____

_____

_____

SUCCESS CRITERIA 15:
TO WRITE AN ADVENTURE STORY

- Include an unfamiliar or dangerous setting, e.g. haunted house, a rainforest, lost in the woods.

- Describe the setting well.

- Include questions to make the reader wonder what is going on, e.g. What was that noise?

- Build the story up to a climax (a part of the story that is really exciting).

- Set the scene and then surprise the reader using connectives like suddenly, without warning, seconds later...

- Include lots of description – use adverbs, adjectives, similes and descriptive phrases.

- Use powerful verbs for impact, e.g. *The wolf <u>pounced</u>* or *The sword <u>pierced</u> his heart.*

- Use adverbs and verbs to show how the main character is feeling, e.g. nervously, hesitantly, surprised, terrified etc.

- Use a range of punctuation.

- Use short and complex sentences.

- Write in paragraphs.

SELF/PEER ASSESSMENT SHEET 15:
TO WRITE AN ADVENTURE STORY

☐ Is the story set in an unfamiliar or dangerous place? e.g. a haunted house, a rainforest, the woods?

☐ Is the setting described well so that the reader can imagine it?

☐ Is there a part of the story that is very exciting?

☐ Are connectives like suddenly, without warning or seconds later used?

☐ Are lots of adjectives used ?

☐ Are adverbs, verbs and descriptive phrases used to show how the main character is feeling, e.g. nervously, terrified etc.

☐ Is a range of punctuation used?

☐ Are short and complex sentences used?

☐ Are paragraphs used?

☐ Does the story have a good last line to end it?

How could this work be improved?

_____

_____

_____

_____

_____

SUCCESS CRITERIA 16:
TO KEEP A READING JOURNAL

- Make detailed notes about the book you are reading.

- Include predictions explaining what you think will happen next at certain points in the story.

- Discuss characters with reference to the text.

- Identify conflicts and dilemmas (problems) the main character faces.

- Explore the use of language in the story. For example, find adjectives, powerful verbs or good descriptive phrases.

- Make notes on the settings in the story.

- Review the story – express your opinion. Say whether you liked the story – why or why not?

- Find evidence from the story to back up your opinions.

SELF/PEER ASSESSMENT SHEET 16:
TO KEEP A READING JOURNAL

☐ Does the journal contain detailed notes about the story?

☐ Are there notes describing first impressions of the story?

☐ Are predictions made (guessing what will happen next)?

☐ Are characters discussed making reference to the text?

☐ Are problems that the main character faces in the story identified and discussed?

☐ Does the journal contain summaries (short explanations of what has happened) of some parts of the story?

☐ Does the journal contain notes on the language used in the story? e.g. adjectives, verbs, descriptive phrases etc.

☐ Does the journal include information about the settings?

☐ At the end of the journal is there a detailed review of the story?

☐ Does the journal include notes about favourite parts of the story?

How could this work be improved?

_____

_____

_____

_____

_____

_____

SUCCESS CRITERIA 17:
TO WRITE A STORY WITH A FLASHBACK

- Use paragraphs.

- Begin in the present time describing current events.

- Use a narrative device to show shifts in time backwards and forwards. For example:
  - Punctuation such as ellipsis (...)
  - Missing a line between paragraphs
  - Using a symbol to divide the text into different sections such as missing a line or stars (* * *) between paragraphs.

- Include phrases alluding to time. For example:
  - That morning...
  - It had started out like any other day...
  - He remembered how things used to be...
  - A few years ago...

- Describe how the main character feels, using a range of adjectives and adverbs.

- Return to the present time at the end of the story.

- To create reader interest, structure the narrative following the sequence of:
  - Problem/feeling of unhappiness or anger
  - Description of how the problem arose (past events)
  - Resolution to problem (or acceptance of change).

SELF/PEER ASSESSMENT SHEET 17:
TO WRITE A STORY WITH A FLASHBACK

☐ Does the story begin in the present time?

☐ Does the story 'flash' backwards into the past in the middle section and then return to the present at the end?

☐ Are there examples of phrases that indicate the passing of time? e.g. earlier that morning, hours later...

☐ Is accurate sentence punctuation used?

☐ Are paragraphs used?

☐ Are descriptions included to indicate how the main character feels at different points in the narrative?

☐ Are a range of adjectives and adverbs used?

☐ Are devices used to indicate shifts in time? For example, ellipsis (...), missing a line or using stars (* * * * *).

☐ Are any problems or unhappy feelings described during the beginning of the story, resolved at the end?

How could this work be improved?

_____

_____

_____

_____

_____

SUCCESS CRITERIA 18:
TO WRITE A BIOGRAPHY

- Write in the past tense.

- Write the title as a question, e.g. Who Was Martin Luther King? or a statement, e.g. The Life of Martin Luther King.

- In the first paragraph explain why the person is famous or important.

- Describe significant events in the person's life.

- Include dates linked to the significant events.

- Write the events in the order in which they occurred.

- Include complex sentences.

- Try to use a range of sentence openers (don't keep starting sentences with he or she).

- In the last paragraph summarise what the person has achieved and (if they are no longer alive) why they should be remembered.

SELF/PEER ASSESSMENT SHEET 18:
TO WRITE A BIOGRAPHY

☐ Is the biography written in the past tense?

☐ Is the title written as a question (e.g. Who Was Martin Luther King?) or a statement (e.g. The Life of Martin Luther King)?

☐ Does the first paragraph explain why the person is famous or important?

☐ Does the biography contain a description of significant events in the person's life?

☐ Does the biography include dates linked to significant events?

☐ Are events written in the order in which they occurred?

☐ Does the text contain complex sentences?

☐ Are a range of sentence openers used (rather than repetitive use of the person's name and he or she)?

☐ Does the last paragraph summarise what the person has achieved and (if they are no longer alive) why they should be remembered?

How could this work be improved?

_____

_____

_____

_____

_____

SUCCESS CRITERIA 19:
TO CONSTRUCT A POINTS OF VIEW CHART

- Plan the layout and design of the chart carefully before you begin, e.g. How many columns and rows will be needed? What about spacing?

- Identify the issue at the top (usually in the form of a question).

- You need 'For' and 'Against' columns.

- List reasons for opinions in the appropriate column.

- State each reason in a clear, precise way using only one sentence.

- Try to write opposing reasons next to each other in the 'For' and 'Against' columns.

- Do not elaborate (add details or evidence) on reasons given.

Optional Features:
End with a statement of own viewpoint at the end.
Use bullet points for each reason.

SELF/PEER ASSESSMENT SHEET 19:
TO CONSTRUCT A POINTS OF VIEW CHART

☐ Is the chart set out clearly and neatly?

☐ Is the issue being debated written at the top?

☐ Are there 'For' and 'Against' columns?

☐ Are reasons for opinions listed in the correct column?

☐ Is each reason written in a clear, precise way?

☐ Is no more than one sentence used for each reason?

☐ Are sentences correctly punctuated?

☐ Are opposing reasons written next to each other in the 'For' and 'Against' columns?

How could this work be improved?

_____

_____

_____

_____

_____

_____

_____

_____

SUCCESS CRITERIA 20:
TO WRITE A DISCUSSION TEXT

- Use a question for the title.

- In the first paragraph identify the issue.

- In the second paragraph discuss reasons and arguments for.*

- In the third paragraph discuss reasons and arguments against.*

- Add to points made using a range of sentence openers, e.g. A further reason..., A further point..., In addition..., Secondly..., Thirdly... etc.

- Use a range of connectives, e.g. however, also, although, consequently, because, but, furthermore, on the other hand, also etc.

- Make reference to statistics or the beliefs and experiences of other people, e.g. Research shows..., Many people believe..., Most children agree that..., The majority of parents feel that... etc.

- In the final paragraph write a conclusion – after weighing up both arguments say what you think.

* This structure is used for writing simple discussion texts. More complex texts may need additional paragraphs to discuss points for and against. Alternatively, the issue could be discussed using the argument followed by counter argument structure.

SELF/PEER ASSESSMENT SHEET 20:
TO WRITE A DISCUSSION TEXT

☐ Is a question used for the title?

☐ Does the first paragraph identify the issue to be discussed?

☐ Does the second paragraph discuss reasons for?

☐ Does the third paragraph discuss reasons against?

☐ Are sentence openers used to add further points to the discussion? e.g. phrases like: A further reason..., A further point..., In addition..., Secondly..., Thirdly... etc.

☐ Is a range of connectives used? e.g. however, also, although, consequently, because, but, furthermore, on the other hand, also etc.

☐ Does the text include reference to statistics or the beliefs and experiences of other people? e.g. Research shows...., Many people believe..., Most children agree that..., The majority of parents feel that... etc.

☐ Does the final paragraph conclude the discussion by stating the viewpoint of the writer (summarising reasons for their view)?

How could this work be improved?

_____

_____

_____

_____

_____

SUCCESS CRITERIA 21:
TO WRITE A PERSUASIVE ARGUMENT

- In the first paragraph identify the issue and your viewpoint.

- In subsequent paragraphs discuss the reason for your view, elaborating on each reason and providing evidence.

- Use a separate paragraph to discuss each reason.

- Use sequencing language to organise your argument, e.g. Firstly, Secondly, Thirdly.

- Use connectives to add to and strengthen your reasons, e.g. in addition, consequently, furthermore, as a result of, because...

- Include statistics or the references to research.

- In the absence of facts use words and phrases which indicate that your opinion is correct, e.g. it is likely that..., it seems unlikely..., most people would agree..., it has been said...

- Use direct, clear language and make strong definitive statements, e.g. It is completely unacceptable to keep wild animals in zoos.

- End with restating your view clearly and summarising the reasons for it.

SELF/PEER ASSESSMENT SHEET 21:
TO WRITE A PERSUASIVE ARGUMENT

☐ Does the first paragraph identify the issue and state the writer's viewpoint?

☐ Are separate paragraphs used to discuss different reasons for the writer's view?

☐ Are reasons elaborated in detail?

☐ Is sequencing language used to organise the argument? e.g. Firstly..., Secondly..., Thirdly...,

☐ Are connectives used to add to and strengthen reasons? e.g. in addition, consequently, furthermore, as a result of, because...

☐ Does the text include reference to statistics or research?

☐ Are phrases used which support the argument? e.g. it is likely that..., most people would agree..., it seems that..., everyone knows...

☐ Are clear, strong, definitive statements made?

☐ Does the text conclude the argument by restating the writer's view and summarising the argument?

How could this work be improved?

_____

_____

_____

_____

_____

SUCCESS CRITERIA 22:
TO WRITE A FORMAL TEXT

- Use precise language.

- Avoid overuse of adjectives and descriptive language.

- State information clearly and specifically.

- Provide all of the necessary information.

- Use a consistent, neat layout.

- Use an impersonal tone – avoiding use of personal pronouns, e.g. you, he, she, they, our, we.

- Include complex sentences.

- Punctuate accurately and appropriately.

- Consider the audience you are writing for, e.g. parents, visitors etc.

SELF/PEER ASSESSSMENT SHEET 22:
TO WRITE A FORMAL TEXT

☐   Is precise, formal language used?

☐   Does the text provide the necessary information?

☐   Is information stated clearly? (So that it can be understood.)

☐   Are very few adjectives included in the text?

☐   Is the text set out very neatly using a consistent layout? (e.g. subsections.)

☐   Is there limited use of personal pronouns (you, he, she, they, our, we)?

☐   Does the text include complex sentences?

☐   Is punctuation accurate and appropriate?

☐   Is the text suitable for the audience it is aimed at? e.g. parents, visitors etc.

How could this work be improved?

_____

_____

_____

_____

_____

_____

_____